Rising Phoenix Martial Arts

Adult Ninjutsu Student Textbook

Rising Phoenix Martial Arts

Adult Ninjutsu Student Textbook

Tom Gillis

Tom Gillis
2016

Copyright © 2016 by F.T.S. Inc.

All rights reserved. This book or any portion thereof may not be reproduced or used in any manner whatsoever without the express written permission of the publisher except for the use of brief quotations in a book review or scholarly journal.

First Printing: 2016

ISBN 978-0-9939421-7-4

F.T.S. Inc.
118 Cimarron Grove Road
Okotoks Alberta Canada T1S 2H1

www.ftsma.com

Ordering Information:

Special discounts are available on quantity purchases by corporations, associations, educators, and others. For details, contact the publisher at the above listed address.

U.S. trade bookstores and wholesalers: Please contact FTS Inc. Tel: (403) 829-7897or email info@ftsma.com

Dedication

For Soke Hatsumi

Table of Contents

Welcome Message 10

Introduction 13

What is Ninjutsu? 15

Dojo Etiquette and Opening/Closing Ceremony 19

Minimum Testing Standards 21

Exam Summaries 23

9th kyu 27

8th kyu 37

7th kyu 45

6th kyu 51

5th kyu 57

4th kyu 63

3rd kyu 67

2nd kyu 75

1st kyu 87

Shodan 95

Testing Forms 97

Welcome Message

Thank you for choosing to train in the Rising Phoenix Martial Arts Adult Ninjutsu Program. I personally believe that martial arts training has the power to transform lives and make it my mission to provide every single student with a transformative experience. That process starts with our Ninja Kids Program and continues in the Juniors Martial Arts Program, and culminates in adult training. There are a few things that will help you understand the program better and help you to get everything out of the training that you can.

The first thing is that at Rising Phoenix we DO NOT focus on technique. This seems like a strange concept to people who are new to training but allow me to elaborate. We focus on PROCESS. The reason for this is simple. I'm not interested in programming clones who can all recite a list of hundreds of techniques. Rather I am interested in helping to develop people to reach their full potential in all aspects of their lives and selves. This means intellectually, physically, and emotionally.

The second thing to keep in mind is that even in a single Ryuha, or school, there is instructor drift. This means that some of the techniques in this book people may have learned by a different name or term or with a slightly different way of doing it.

Lastly in order to help me achieve my goal, that is developing you, the training mustn't stop at the dojo. It is the students responsibility to get to class, listen and work hard, and think about the lessons at home and continue to train at home. If a student brings their commitment to the table they will see results.

I hope you enjoy the book and the training and can't wait to see you on the mats.

Tom Gillis

Introduction to Rising Phoenix Martial Arts

At Rising Phoenix our Adult Ninjutsu program focuses on Bujinkan Budo Taijutsu as transmitted by Dr. Masaaki Hatsumi. It is our goal to make martial arts training available to people from all walks of life. Although our program is based in Bujinkan it also borrows from many other martial arts such as Wrestling, Brazilian Jiu Jitsu, Arnis, Jeet Kune Do, and Muay Thai Kickboxing.

The instructors use a variety of tools for teaching martial arts. These tools include, but aren't limited to, literary resources, video sources, lecture, social networking and online resources, and demonstration of skill. It is our goal to engage students on several different levels to maximize learning and provide the student with a positive experience that helps them reach their potential and enjoy the learning process. We strive for a positive atmosphere where all students feel welcome regardless of age, ability, gender, ethnicity, or religious beliefs.

Introduction to the Training

The Phoenix represents rebirth in western culture and in Japanese culture represents the sun, fidelity, prosperity, and obedience. The phoenix is a very important and personal symbol to Sensei Tom Gillis who created Rising Phoenix Martial Arts. It means a constant drive to move forwards and not be held back by our mistakes or fears or self doubts. It represents Shugyo, constantly striving to improve ourselves and constantly being reborn as a better version of ourselves, moving towards our ultimate potential.

At Rising Phoenix Martial Arts the Ninja Kids program focuses on learning martial arts through play, learning social values and relationships, learning martial arts values, and anti-bullying.

We use the same rank structure as designed by Kanō Jigorō (嘉納 治五郎, 28 October 1860 – 4 May 1938) and encourages students to study and train hard to move through the ranks. The dojo is a contact dojo where students strike, grapple, and throw each other. When possible and safe to do so students are exposed to live training weapons. A constant reinforcement of *Bujin*, warrior spirit, is taught. To develop a true *Bujin*, or *Bujutsu* (warrior technique) students must experience reality training.

My belief is that martial arts training is for everyone, not only the gifted athletes but for the everyday person. Students aren't held to the same standards as each other, but rather are measured according to their own potential for excellence.

Sensei Tom has a direct lineage to Dr. Masaaki Hatsumi, current *Soke* of the 9 traditions and founder of the Bujinkan System. His first instructor was Orlando Sensei who presented him with his *shodan* (black belt), followed by *Shihan* Jay Creasey who he currently trains with and who presented him with his *sandan* (3rd degree black belt). Tom trains with other shihan's as well and attends training in Japan to learn directly from Soke Hatsumi who promoted him to *godan* (5th degree black belt) in January 2014.

Training in a martial arts system such as Bujinkan Budo Tai Jutsu requires patience and repetition. The goal of the Ninja Kids program is to interest kids in martial arts from an early age. Techniques from various martial arts are taught, not just Ninjutsu. This also means that not all drills have a direct technical application. Some exercises are designed to strengthen the body, some are designed to improve mind-body connection, and some are designed to teach relaxation, some co-ordination. This is important to keep in mind when training.

What is Ninjutsu?

By Sensei Tom Gillis

The term Ninjutsu is often misunderstood and misused. In fact what ninjutsu means is "the offensive and defensive system of persevering." That's quit the mouthful. Basically ninjutsu is different for everyone who practices it. Shihan Jay once said "there's Hatsumi Sensei's Ninjutsu, Canadian Ninjutsu, and your ninjutsu." What this means is that each individual is on their own journey and because Ninjutsu focus' on process we can each experience it in our own way.

For the most part today's Ninjutsu is transmitted through the Bujinkan. This is a particular system that was created by Dr. Masaaki Hatsumi. He is the grandmaster of 9 unique martial arts systems that he combined to create the Bujinkan. These 9 systems were each their own school, or Ryuha in Japanese, and throughout the course of history were brought together through familial alliances and bonds. Some of the schools were samurai lineage, and some were of ninja origin. Ninjutsu itself didn't emerge as a martial art until after the Tokugawa shogunate in the early 1600's. Before that it existed as stealth training and before that as the philosophy Ninpo, which can actually be found in military records from many different martial arts systems including Ju Jutsu, Karate, Kenjutsu, and other fighting systems of ancient Japan.

Takamatsu sensei was the first person to be the soke (grandmaster) in all 9 and he passed the lineages to Hatsumi sensei. Takamatsu sensei used to train the schools independent of each other and would instruct that a particular kata or movement was from a particular school and their names. Hatsumi sensei however blended all 9 into the Bujinkan, sometimes known as Hatsumi Han (Hatsumi house or system). The idea being that a student would learn a certain level of freedom and expression by seamlessly transitioning from 1 style to the next without thinking of it as a "style".

The 9 schools are;

Togakure Ryu, Hidden Door School. As with most of Ninjutsu the Togakure Ryu is shrouded in mystery. Of the nine schools in Bujinkan this school is the oldest and the foundation. Up until the year 2000 most training certificates said "Togakure Ryu" on them and not "Bujinkan."

The Ryuha is thought to have developed in the late 1100's/early 1200's when a samurai retainer, Daisuke Nishina, escaped a battle where his forces were defeated and killed, and fled into the mountains of Iga. There he evaded capture and met a group of monks from China who trained in martial arts on Mount Hiei-zan. He took refuge with them and combined their spiritual training with his own, and their martial art with his own samurai arts. He developed a system of training to defeat samurai and that focused on 18 disciplines.

It wasn't until 3 generations after its creation that the system was formalized and the name "Hidden Door School" was created. The name itself eludes to the philosophy of finding the path less travelled and the using the unsuspected strategy to defeat an opponent. Training in the Togakure Ryu could take a lifetime to learn all the different skills!

Gyokko Ryu, Jeweled Tiger School. This school is believed to have been brought to Japan from China by Cho Gyokko during the Tang Dynasty. The school teaches kosshijutsu, which calls for attacks to the muscles and nerve points of the body, shitojutsu or using the thumbs and fingers for striking and included styles of sword and stick fighting. This Ryu favors circular movement and is one half of a complete fighting system, the other half being linear fighting found in the Koto Ryu.

Koto Ryu, Tiger Knocking Down School. This school is the sister style to Gyokko-ryu. The school is very linear and favours straight lines as opposed to circular motions. This style of fighting uses kempo (short fist striking) and koppojutsu or "bone law art" which can be broken down into three elements. The first is breaking bones, the second is destroying joints, and the third is manipulating an opponent's skeleton so that they can't maintain balance. This style of fighting is believed to have been brought from Korea to Japan by a monk named Chan Busho. Many movements resemble knife fighting and short blade combat.

Kukishinden, Transmission of the 9 Demon Gods School. This school is often described as a battlefield school. Many of the movements take into account body armour and the strategy is often to unbalance your opponent to knock them on their backs. From here a sword or other weapon could've been employed to finish a confrontation. The Kukishinden teaches unarmed fighting (taijutsu), and favours swords (ken jutsu), spears (so jutsu) and short staffs (hanbo jutsu) along with supplemental military strategy and other minor ninjutsu skills.

Kumogakure Ryu, Hidden In Clouds School. This *ryu* teaches many taijutsu methods of leaping and uses a specialty spear with a hook that was used as a combat tool and to climb ships. As with all Ninja schools strategy and mind set are favoured and emphasized over fighting ability. The warriors of this school used armored sleeves to deflect blades and confuse enemies and wore demon masks to frighten and distract them. The sleeves and shin armour usually would've been made out of bo shuriken (throwing spikes) or sanban shuriken (throwing stars) sewn into pockets on the boots or gauntlets. Not only could they deflect weapons but also be accessed as a weapon to launch at opponents or hit and cut with the weapons in the clothing. It's thought that many of the originators of this school were employed on ships and fishing vessels as protection against pirates and that's why the movements have a gentle swaying motion.

Gikan Ryu, School of truth, loyalty and justice. This school also teaches koppojutsu, the system of unarmed fighting to break bones, joints, or disrupt balance. This school is said to have been developed by a student of the Gyokko-ryu and Koto-ryu and basically combines the strategies and movements of both into his own unique way of moving and fighting. The teachings of the school are very secretive and not taught publically. Many believe the school favoured hidden sword (biken) techniques for its primary weapon. The lineage of this school is in debate and Soke Masaaki Hatsumi's claim that he is the current grandmaster is challenged by Shoto Tanemura. What we do know is that an underlying philosophy in the school was to keep the peace and to never attack first, but rather to use your skill only in defense.

Shinden Fudo Ryu, immovable heart school. This art has two styles of unarmed combat, Jutaijutsu (grappling methods) and Daken Taijutsu (striking methods), although it's believed that originally the school only taught striking methods and it wasn't until much later that the grappling techniques were introduced from another source.

Gyokishin Ryu, Jeweled Heart School. Gyokishin mainly concentrates on the espionage skills and other abilities of the ninja than fighting. It is considered a "secret" school and Soke Hatsumi doesn't disclose its teachings.

Takagi Yoshin Ryu Jutaijutsu, High Tree Raised Heart School. This Ryuha is a system of Ju Jutsu (grappling techniques) which teaches fast breaks, submissions, ground fighting and chokes. In the upper levels of training it is practiced while wearing samurai swords and sometimes employs long staffs as weapons. The school is thought to have been developed for body guards and specializes in applying the grappling techniques with speed so that an opponent cannot counter.

Each of the 9 schools are battlefield arts, meaning that as well as the technical aspects of the school there is an underlying philosophy of tactics and awareness. In many of the kata's from all the schools a turning movement is used (sometimes at the very end) to circumnavigate your surroundings or angles are sought to use opponents against each other. In each of the 9 weapon skills are taught at the very beginning of the training and continue throughout. This is because many of the body movements take into account the idea that soldiers were trained in weapons first so they were already familiar with moving as though they were armed. Soldiers only fought empty handed in the case of an emergency.

As you can see from the descriptions of the 9 Ryuha of the Bujinkan there is a wide diversity and range of skills. Any one of these 9 schools was, and could still be, taught on its own and a student could spend a lifetime exploring just 1 and mastering its techniques, principles, philosophies, and movements.

Dojo Etiquette and Opening/Closing Ceremony

Students are expected to keep in mind at all times the ideas of respect and discipline and do their best to demonstrate and follow dojo protocol and etiquette. Our protocol is slightly less strict than what students may find in Japan or other Bujinkan dojo's. Proper dojo etiquette is as follows;

1. **Bowing when stepping on or off mats.** Students are only required to bow when first stepping onto the mats before class begins and at the end of class when they're heading out to the change room or leaving for the session. Students aren't required to bow when entering or leaving the training area for breaks, to fetch equipment, or for first aid. To bow properly before training stand at the edge of the mats, look at the kamidana and bow from the waist keeping the head and eyes up. Then step onto the mats with the left foot. At the end of training proceed to an edge of the mat with heels on the edge, look at the kamidana and bow from the waist head and eyes up. Step off the mat right foot first.

2. **Bowing to each other.** When beginning training for the first time with a new partner or partners give each other a brief bow from the waist with head and eyes up looking at each other. Repeat when moving onto another partner. Bowing to the same partner isn't required when an instructor requests the group to come in for demonstration or when resuming training after demonstrations, breaks, or fetching equipment. If requested to provide a class demonstration enter the designated training space with your partner or partners and bow to each other. Perform the demonstrations until directed to stop. Bow to each other again and exit the demonstration area.

3. **Bowing to instructors.** Similar to bowing to each other, if an instructor requests training or uke bow to each other before the demonstration. Perform the required number of demonstrations. Bow to each other and exit the demonstration area. If an instructor observes a performance or training issue during practice and quickly interrupts the group bowing is not required.

4. **Hygiene.** Keep uniforms and equipment cleaned and maintained, finger and toe nails trim, and clean hands and feet before class. Do your best to keep the mats and training area clean and free from debris, dirt, and blood. It is the students responsibility to keep the dojo clean. Students not following hygiene protocols may be excluded from training. This is to keep our environment clean so that students don't get sick.

5. **Uniforms.** Students are expected to wear all patches on their uniforms. This includes rank patch(es), Dojo membership patch, and a Canadian flag. Other patches may be worn at sensei Tom's (or designates) discretion. In the summer kekogi tops may be replaced with t-shirts.

6. **Equipment.** Always ask someone else's permission before handling their equipment. Pass equipment to each other respectfully and with care. Do not toss or throw equipment to each other unless as part of an exercise.

7. **Late arrival.** Late arrivals are not viewed as disrespectful if for reasonable reason (i.e. work, traffic, confusion in location, etc.). Students are requested to do their best to be on time for every training session AND to and from breaks and fetching equipment. In case of being late for class proceed to and edge of the training space, leave your feet off the mat and sit in seiza no kamae with knees on the mat. Wait for an instructor to acknowledge you and invite you onto the mat. Follow proper protocol for entering the training space at that time.

8. **Opening and closing ceremony.** When training is beginning for the night the instructor will ask everyone in attendance to line up facing the kamidana. Students line up facing the kamidana in order or rank from left to right with the most senior student far left. There is room for 12 students in the front row with the space immediately in front of the kamidana reserved for instructor(s). If there's more than 12 students in attendance then begin other row's as necessary following the same formula. If your kekogi needs adjusting turn away from the kamidana, make the adjustment, and turn back. Follow the instructors instructions to either sit in seiza no kamae or stand and assume gassho no kamae. If seated in seiza no kamae follow any instructions until the instructor requests the gassho position. The instructor will say "shiken haramitsu daikomyio." As a group all the students repeat the mantra. Then as a big group everyone claps twice and bows to the kamidana, sit or stand straight up again, clap once and bow again. The student on the far left will say "sensei ni rei" at which time everyone bows to the kamidana together and says "onegaishimasu." The instructor will provide any discussions or instructions and class begins. At the end of class the exact same ceremony is conducted except that the last saying becomes "arigato onegaishimasu."

Adult Ninjutsu Minimum Testing Standards

Students are evaluated in 3 areas of competency. They are *taijutsu*, the ability to move and use the body, *general knowledge*, tested through written exams, demonstrations, and reading kanji, and the third and final aspect is *budo*, the way of the warrior, tested through dojo etiquette and behavior.

In order to apply for a rank test the student must meet a minimum number of hours since beginning training. Hours are applied from attending class or private training sessions at a 1-to-1 ratio, attending other sanctioned Bujinkan Training Events at a 1-to-1 ratio, attending other sanctioned Non- Bujinkan events at a 2-to-1 ratio and assisting as *Uke* for special events or children's classes at a 2-to-1 ratio. **Just because the minimum number of hours are met does not mean that the test will be successful.** Following is a list of the minimum training hours required for a rank. Ranks may be awarded by Sensei Tom or his designate solely at his discretion. Once a rank is awarded it is not to be questioned by other students or instructors. Rank may be revoked by Sensei Tom or his designate at any time.

Rank	Total Number of Training Hours for Minimum Eligibility
9 kyu	54
8 kyu	108
7 kyu	162
6 kyu	270
5 kyu	378
4 kyu	486
3 kyu	648
2 kyu	810
1 kyu	972
Shodan	1188
2 dan	1620
3 dan	2268
4 dan	3132
5 dan	4212

Each exam is accumulative, meaning that students must re-demonstrate all the previous material AS WELL AS any new material. Although Ninjutsu does not have to follow a linear progression in skill development, the exams were created to encourage a feeling of flow from one skill to the next. The goal in developing the exams was to build a curriculum that set a foundation and then continued to build on that foundation.

Each exam also includes Kanji. Kanji are Japanese characters that originated in China. Kanji are hieroglyphics (pictures and symbols) which represent entire words and concepts. Many times students question why they have to learn the kanji. As a student progresses through ninjutsu eventually they will reach a point where to continue to develop they must challenge themselves to learn a deeper understanding of concepts. Because the kanji are symbols that are thousands of years old they can help lead a student to this deeper understanding. As well Soke Hatsumi doesn't speak or publish in English. Having a basic understanding of Japanese Martial Arts terms will help students recognize words and skills and later on be able to conduct their own research and read material from Japan.

A few notes understanding testing:

Once a student has met the attendance requirements and feel like they know the material on an exam they can submit for the exam. The student simply fills out and hands in the score sheet for that exam. At the end of every 3 month quarter exams are conducted.

On the day of the exam the examiner will call the student up to the center of the room and begin asking them to show the skills and kata on the score sheet. Each skill is worth a possible 1 mark. If the student performs the skill at a skill level appropriate for their level they receive 1 mark. If they perform the skill but with body mechanics that the examiner feels are not adequate for their rank then they will receive 1/2 mark. If the student can't perform the skill or performs the skill in a completely ineffective manner then a mark of 0 is recorded. At the end of the exam students are required to have an 80% (80/100) to receive a passing grade.

In the event a student fails an exam they can retake the exam at the end of the next quarter.

Understanding the Self Defense Criteria

At each test students are required to demonstrate self defense kata's that they've created and rehearsed. The self defense kata's are demonstrated on the right and the left. Kata's that start with the uke touching the tori are demonstrated blindfolded. Kata's that don't start with the uke and tori touching each other are demonstrated with compromised or impaired vision, usually in the form of oil smeared across safety glasses. The self defense kata's are marked using 6 criteria. They are Precision, Timing, Balance, Co-ordination, Power, and Tactical Effectiveness.

Exam Summaries

White Belt Levels
Focus on Kihon Waza (fundamental skills)

9th (kyuu) Kyu (Bujin Patch red circle white kanji & white obi)

1. Belt tying, Opening and Closing Ceremony and Written Exam
2. Read Kanji: Nin 忍
3. Demonstrate an understanding of the RPMA core values, dojo etiquette, and budo
4. Taihenjutsu Ukemi Gata: Zenpo Ryoho (forwards), Koho (rearwards), sayu yoko zenpo (sliding sidefall)
5. kamae: seiza (formal seated), fudoza (immovable seated), shizen (natural), hira (turning flat), hoko (entrapping bear), hicho (rising bird), doko (angry tiger), ichimonji (number 1), jumonji (number 10), kosei (advancing), bobie (prepared), and ihen (rapidly changing)
6. Self defense: 1 mei tsuki, 1 mei geri, 1 lapel grab
7. Randori: 10 attacks in line

8th (hachi) Kyu (1 white star and white obi)

1. Read Kanji: Bu 武 and Jin 神
2. Demonstrate an understanding of the RPMA core values, dojo etiquette, and budo
3. taihenjutsu ukemi gata: zenpo kaiten (front roll), koho kaiten (back roll), yoko kaiten (side roll), and oten ukemi (cartwheel)
4. 16 jewels
5. kihon happo: ura gyaku (inside wristlock)
6. Self Defense: 3 mei tsuki, 2 mei geri, 2 lapel grab
7. Randori: 20 circular in order

7th (shichi) Kyu (2 white stars and white obi)

1. Read Kanji: Po 法 Do 道 and Jutsu 術
2. Demonstrate an understanding of the RPMA core values, dojo etiquette, and budo
3. Sanshin no Kata and Kihon Happo: Chi no kata, Sui no kata, Ka no kata, Fu no kata, Ku no kata (Earth, water, fire, air, void forms)
4. Self defense: 4 mei tsuki, 2 mei geri, 2 lapel grab, 1 te hodoki
5. Randori: 30 circle random order

Green Belt Levels
Focus on hodoki waza (escaping skills)

6th (roku) Kyu (3 white stars & green obi)

1. Read Kanji: : Ki 気, Kara 空, Shi 士, Hou 鳳
2. Demonstrate an understanding of the RPMA core values, dojo etiquette, and budo
3. Kihon Happo: omote gyaku, ura gyaku, omote no tsui,
4. tai hodoki (body escapes): pyramid, breast stroke, isometric tension, knuckle grind
5. Green belt stress test
6. Self defense: 5 mei tsuki, 2 mei geri, 2 lapel grab, 2 te hodoki, 1 tai hodoki, 1 nage hodoki
7. randori: 40 with stick, knife, firearm

5th (go) Kyu (4 white stars and green obi)

1. Read Kanji: Ju 柔, Go 剛, Jo 場, Kan 館, 者 Sha
2. Demonstrate an understanding of the RPMA core values, dojo etiquette, and budo
3. Kihon Happo: ichimonji kata (form #1), jumonji kata (#10 form)
4. te hodoki: opening lotus, elbow pressure, prayer to heaven, takagi yoshin omote gyaku, moving the bail of rice
5. Self defense: 5 mei tsuki, 2 mei geri, 2 lapel grab, 2 te hodoki, 1 tai hodoki, 1 nage hodoki, 1 newaza
6. randori: 50 attacks with stick, knife, firearm

4th (yon) Kyu (1 gold stars and green obi)

1. Read Kanji: Koshi 腰, Hiza 膝, Hiji 肘, Ashi 足, , Tai 体, Te 手
2. Demonstrate an understanding of the RPMA core values, dojo etiquette, and budo
3. Kihon Happo: hicho no kata (rising bird form)
4. aruki waza: neko aruki (cat walk), shinobi aruki (stealth walk), hirai aruki (sweep walk), kou aruki (crane walk), ushiro aruki (rearwards walking), hajai aruki (fast walk)
5. Self defense: 6 mei tsuki, 3 mei geri, 3 lapel grab, 3 te hodoki, 2 tai hodoki, 2 nage hodoki, 2 newaza
6. randori: 60 attacks with stick, knife, firearm

Brown Belt Levels
Focus on Connecting Waza

3rd (san) Kyu (2 gold stars and brown obi)

1. Read Kanji: Rei 礼, Makoto 誠, Jin 仁, Yuki 勇氣, Gi 義, Meiyo 名誉, Chugi 忠義
2. Demonstrate an understanding of the RPMA core values, dojo etiquette, and budo
3. Kihon Happo: oni kudaki (figue 4 grip shoulder lock)
4. ne waza (ground fighting): ebi (shrimp), ura ebi (reverse shrimp), yoko ebi (side shrimp), upa (bridge), scissor kick, scissor sweep, turtle, pyramid
5. Self defense: 7 mei tsuki, 4 mei geri, 4 lapel grab, 4 te hodoki, 3 tai hodoki, 3 nage hodoki, 3 newaza
6. Brown belt stress test
7. randori: 70 attacks with weapons and multiple opponent

2nd (ni) Kyu (3 gold stars and brown obi)

1. Kanji: Shirabe 調, Moguri 潜, Sabaki 捌, Hei 兵, In 陰, Yo 陽, Kyo 強, Jyaku 弱
2. Demonstrate an understanding of the RPMA core values, dojo etiquette, and budo
3. Kihon Happo: musha dori (inside shoulder lock)
4. Nage Waza (throws and takedowns): Ganseki Nage, Ganseki Nage Henka (yoko), Ganseki Goshi, Harai Goshi, O'Soto Gari, O'Soto Nage, Tomoe Nage, Temakura, Sui Ryu, Yoko Nagare Henka, Yoko Nagare Henka 2, Yoko Nagare Henka 3 (ushiro), Kata Garuma, Double Leg Shot, O' Gyaku Kata
5. Self defense: 8 mei tsuki, 5 mei geri, 4 lapel grab, 4 te hodoki, 3 tai hodoki, 4 nage hodoki, 4 newaza
8. randori: 80 attacks with weapons and multiple opponent

1st (ichi) Kyu (3 gold stars and brown obi)

1. Kanji: Waza 技, Chi 地, Sui 水, Ka 火, Fu 風, Ken 拳, Ken 剣, Ai 合, Hodoki 解
2. Demonstrate an understanding of the RPMA core values, dojo etiquette, and budo

3. Buki waza: ken jutsu, bo Jutsu, hanbo Jutsu, tanto jutsu, shuriken jutsu, kusari jutsu
4. Self defense: 9 mei tsuki, 5 mei geri, 4 lapel grab, 4 te hodoki, 4 tai hodoki, 4 nage hodoki, 5 newaza
5. randori: 90 with weapons and multiple opponent

Shodan (Bujin Patch red circle black kanji & black obi)

1. Read Kanji: Ryu 龍, Tora 虎, Take 竹, Zen 禅, Shugyo 修行, Nagare 流, Sensei 先生, Shidoshi 指道者, Shihan 師範, Soke 宗家宗家
2. Demonstrate an understanding of the RPMA core values, dojo etiquette, and budo
3. Self Defense: : 10 mei tsuki, 6 mei geri, 5 lapel grab, 5 te hodoki, 5 tai hodoki, 5 nage hodoki, 5 newaza
4. Randori: 100 attacks with weapons and multiple opponent

9 th Kyu

Introduction

The 9th kyu exam is intended to get students used to testing in a martial arts program. The purpose of the 9th kyu material is to teach students the fundamental postures and how to fall properly. This will help protect them during training and also in real life in case of slips, trips, and other falls.

Kanji

The kanji for 9th kyu 忍 is pronounced "nin". It is the core of Ninjutsu, Ninja, and Ninpo. It is the most important concept for a student of the ninja arts. Nin originally meant "stealing in". In modern terms we would use the term "stealth". It has also become known to mean "perseverance".

Technique #1. Zenpo Ryoho Ukemi

1. Zenpo ryoho is the first fall learned. It is a front fall while distributing the impact over both arms. Zenpo means forwards and ryoho means "both arms".
2. To practice the front fall stand in shizen no kamae and make a triangle shaped frame in front of you with both arms. (fig.1)
3. Next bend the knees slightly and drop and fall forwards. Be sure to keep the eyes up to help keep the face from hitting the ground. (fig.2)
4. Impact should be made on the ground with the arms **ONLY** while landing on the triangle from the tips of the fingers to the elbow of both arms at the same time. The timing is critical. The entire triangle frame impacts the ground at the same time. The body and knees do not touch the ground. (fig.3 &4)

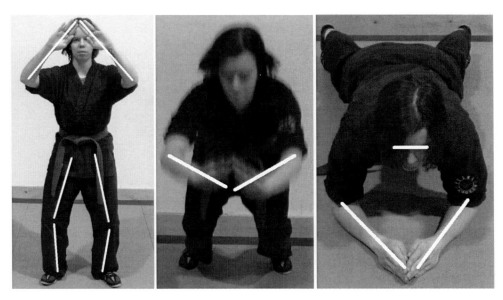

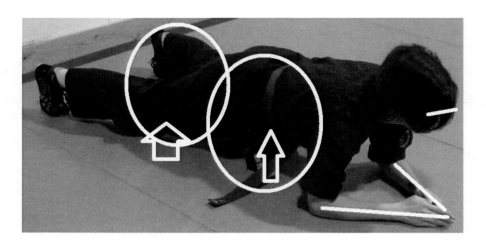

Technique #2. Ukemi Gata Koho

1. Koho denotes rearwards falling.
2. Like the front fall the goal is to spread out the impact across a large surface area comprised of large weight bearing bones and skeletal muscle.
3. To practice the technique extend 1 leg forwards and off the ground. Cant the body slightly to that side. (fig.1)
4. Use the post leg to control the decent to the ground. Be sure to keep the hands and chin tucked to the chest. (fig. 2)
5. Land on the buttocks of the extended leg. The hands and chin are tucked to the chest and the eyes are looking forwards. (fig. 3)
6. Tuck both knees to the chest to absorb the last bit of kinetic energy and protect the legs from an assailant. Keep the back of the head off the ground, eyes forwards, and chin tucked. (fig.4)

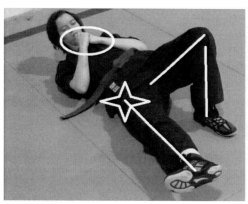
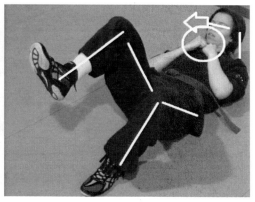

Technique #3. Ukemi Gata Yoko

1. The word yoko means sideways. This technique is a sideways fall.
2. Like before the goal is to spread out the impact across a large surface area comprised of large weight bearing bones and skeletal muscle.
3. Extend one leg off the ground and across the body to the opposite side. (fig.1)
4. Drop down and towards the side of the extended leg controlling the fall with the posted leg. (fig. 2)
5. Extend the arm out upon impact so that the body makes and L shape. Contact with the ground is made first with the buttock of the extended leg and second with the inside of the extended arm. (fig. 3)

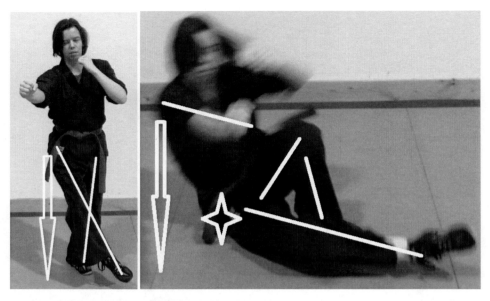

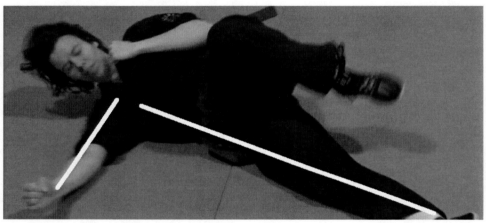

Technique #4. Shizen no kamae

1. Shizen no kamae translates to "natural posture". It is the starting posture to move in and out of any of the other kamae.
2. From shizen no kamae movement can be in any direction, including angles and up and down.
3. In shizen the shoulders are over the hips, which are over the knees, which are over the ankles. Weight is distributed equally on each foot. The fee are shoulder width apart and the knees are slightly bent.

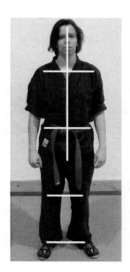

Technique #5. Seiza no Kamae

1. Seiza no Kamae means "formal seated posture" and is used in formal situations such as listening to instruction or receiving directions, awards, and other formal meetings. It is used in the dojo in the same circumstances. The word "kamae" however denotes that it can also be used for and during movement. Seiza no kamae is an important posture in kenjutsu (sword arts) and in ne waza (ground fighting).
2. To perform seiza no kamae slide the right foot backwards and lower down onto the right knee. Next slide the left foot back until the left knee is on the ground also. Lastly sit back on the feet, straighten the back, and widen the knees.
3. Students should be able to get up and down from shizen to seiza without putting their hands on the ground. This is done primarily through shifting weight from side to side and extending hips forwards while standing.

Technique #6. Fudoza no Kamae

1. Fudoza means "immovable seat" and can be used in less formal circumstances than seiza. From seiza shift slightly to one side and adjust the other leg so that it is folded in front and underneath the body.
2. Students should be able to move from seiza to fudoza without putting their hands on the ground. This is achieved through understanding how to shift the weight laterally while making the transitions.

Technique #7. Hira no Kamae

1. Hira no kamae means "turning flat posture" and is a kamae used for moving out of the way of incoming straight line attacks suck as overhead chops, thrusts, and straight punches. In modern combative systems it's usually referred to as "opening the door" because the

body swings rearwards from a pivot point to allow the attack to pass by.
2. Once finished the hands are raised and extended, the eyes are fixed to the threat, and the body and legs should be in line with each other. (fig. 1)

Technique #8. Hoko no Kamae

1. Hoko no kamae is most accurately translated as "entrapping bear posture." While it's originally taught as a receiving posture to pull the torso back out of the way of mid level thrusting attacks students will later learn how to use it as an attacking and trapping posture.
2. To perform hoko no kamae slide rearwards on the feet while pulling the navel back and shooting the arms out and up. When finished the arc of the arms from a bend in the elbows should make a circular shape. (fig. 1)

Technique #9. Hicho no Kamae

1. Hicho no Kamae (bird posture) is taught defensively to clear a lead leg from an incoming low attack. It can however be used offensively to load isometric tension for kicking and leaping.
2. To begin slide rearwards as in Hoko no Kamae but leave both arms in front of the chest, one tucked close and one extended to intercept incoming high level attacks. Next pull the lead leg knee up and touch the foot to the rear leg calf. (fig. 1)

Technique #10. Ichimonji no Kamae

1. Ichimonji no Kamae means "#1 posture" and denotes linear movement and straight arms. While it may be used for advancing an attack or defense it is first learned as a defensive (receiving) posture.
2. From Shizen no Kamae slide 1 leg rearwards and raise that hand to cover the heart. The hand corresponding to the forwards leg also raises to chest level but stays extended. Both knees are bent and the rear knee and foot turns to 90 degrees. The front toes and knee should point at a

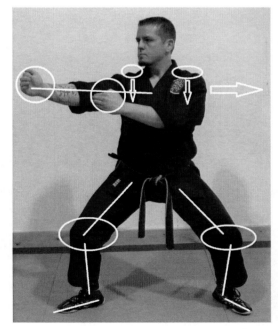

forwards target. Both knees should be directly over the feet and not collapsed inwards. More weight is placed on the rearwards leg. The spine is erect and shoulders relaxed. (fig. 1)

Technique #11. Bobi no Kamae

1. Bobi no Kamae means "prepared defensive posture" and is thought to be used for accessing a weapon from the obi (belt).
2. From Ichimonji no Kamae drop the rear hand to the belt/hip. (fig. 1)

Technique #12. Ihen no Kamae

1. Ihen no Kamae means "rapidly changing posture" and is the most difficult posture to learn due to the complex body mechanics involved. It is regarded as an attacking posture.
2. From Shizen no Kamae begin by stepping forwards deep onto 1 leg. This forwards knee should be bent and in line with the foot. It may extend over the foot.
3. The rear leg should straighten as it pushes into the ground and both feet should point forwards.
4. The hand corresponding with the lead leg strikes out and forwards while maintaining a slight bend in the elbow.
5. The rear hand drops to the hips.
6. The shoulders rotate rearwards to turn the body 90 degrees in relation to the target. While turning the shoulders however the knees must still line up with the feet and the eyes remain fixed on the target.

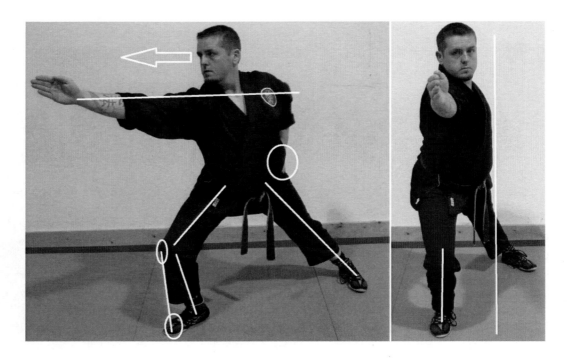

Technique #13. Jumonji no Kamae

1. Jumonji no Kamae means "number ten posture" which emphasizes an advancing posture with arms crossed. The number 10 in Japanese is two crossed lines.
2. From Shizen no Kamae begin by stepping forwards and cross the arms.
3. The arm corresponding with the lead leg should be the one crossed on top.
4. be sure to keep the shoulders relaxed and down, eyes forwards on the target, knees slightly bent, and both feet point towards the attacker.

Technique #14. Kosei no Kamae

1. Kosei no Kamae means "advancing posture".
2. From Jumonji no Kamae uncross the arms so the forwards arm lifts and clears high and the inside arm presses and clears low.
3. Be sure to keep the shoulders relaxed and down, eyes forwards on the target, knees slightly bent, and both feet point towards the attacker.

Technique #15. Doko no Kamae

1. Doko no Kamae means "angry tiger posture" which emphasizes an obtuse angle to an incoming attack, a low posture, and building isometric tension through the body (like a cat in ambush about to pounce).
2. From Shizen no Kamae begin by stepping rearwards and on an angle with one leg. Slide the other leg slightly back along the same angle.
3. The arm corresponding with the lead leg should be raise up to chest level.
4. The rear hand gets pulled up to the ear and the shoulder blades are squeezed together.
5. Like in ichimonji no kamae the knees should line up with the feet.
6. There are two hand positions represented. Either are acceptable.

8 th Kyu

Introduction

The hachikyu (8th kyu) material is designed to help students understand the progressing from falls to rolls and presents the 16 Treasured Fists. When combined with the kamae learned previously the 16 Jewels represent the fundamental methods in which to strike.

Kanji

The 8th kyu kanji's are Bu 武 and Jin 神. Bu translates to *Warrior* and Jin means *Spirit*. Together they appear on the patch that students wear over their heart after successfully completing their 9th kyu exam. This is the universal symbol of Bujinkan students worldwide.

Technique #1. Zenpo Kaiten Ryote

1. Zenpo kaiten ryote is a forwards shoulder roll where both hands are placed on the ground during the decent part of the roll.
2. to begin squat down to the ground and place both hands on the ground. The squat is achieved by flaring the knees out wide. Be sure to keep the eyes up and feel the ground with your hands and feet. (fig. 1)
3. Turn slightly to one side and put the opposite knee on the ground. Begin lower the torso to the ground and tilt the head in the direction of the body rotation. For example, if turning to the right the right ear touches the right shoulder, the left knee touches the ground, and the left arm flattens on the ground . At this stage the eyes should still be looking forwards. (fig. 2)
4. Continue to round the back and lower shoulder to the ground. Once the shoulder makes contact tuck into a tight ball and roll forwards towards a target. Make sure that contact with the ground is diagonal across the back from a shoulder to the opposite hip. Looking up at the sky under the arm not making contact with the ground will assist in keeping the head out of the way and rounding the back. (fig. 3)
5. Finish the roll in a 3 point kneeling posture with the hands and eyes up. (fig. 4)

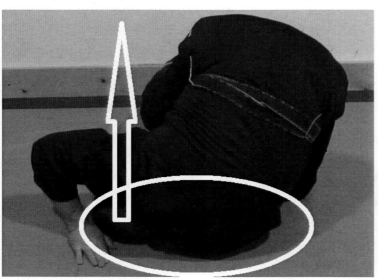
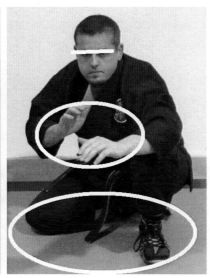

Technique #2. Koho Kaiten

1. Kohon kaiten is a rearwards shoulder roll. Because of the anatomy of the head in comparison to the body at younger ages most children find it easier to learn. It begins with the back fall (see 9th kyu) and changes at the point the knees are tucked to the chest.
2. If landing with the right leg extended, touch the right ear to the right shoulder thereby exposing the left shoulder. The roll is going to make contact with the ground from the right buttock diagonal across the back to the left shoulder. To facilitate this tuck the right knee over the left shoulder. (fig. 1)
3. The tucked leg (in the example above the left) has a shorter rotation and will make contact with the ground first. (fig. 2)
4. Finish the roll in a 3 point kneeling posture facing the same direction as before rolling. (fig. 3)

Technique #3. Yoko Kaiten

1. Yoko kaiten (sideways rolling) starts at the point the body has made contact with the ground on one side and is in an "L" shape.
2. The extended leg is going to act as a pendulum by swinging over the head and body laterally. Be sure to keep the eyes looking forwards at a target. (fig. 1 & 2)
3. Finish in a 3 point kneeling posture The eyes and hands are up. (fig. 3)

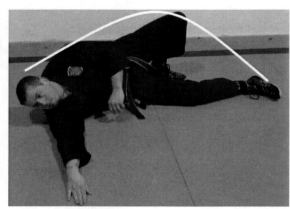

16 Jewels

Fudo Ken

Fudo Ken means "Immovable Fist" or a basic closed fist. Although it can be performed at various elevations depending on the goal it is first learned it at a high level aimed directly for the opponents face.

Boshi Ken

Boshi Ken is when the thumb and index knuckle protrude slightly forwards. It is designed to strike at soft targets and pressure points.

Shuto

Shuto is a strike with the blade of the hand. The blade of the hand is the meaty part right below the pinky finger. To make the shuto the hand starts as a fist and opens into a "scoop" shape just before impact. The thumb and the fingers are squeezed tight (imagine scooping water into the palm of the hand and not letting any leak out between the fingers). Ura shuto is when this strike is delivered with the palm down, in a back hand fashion. Omote shuto is delivered in a forehand fashion. The palm should be facing up when completed.

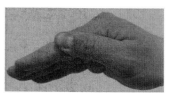

Koppo Ken

Koppo Ken means "bone method fist" and is used from a sideways striking motion. To make koppo ken start with fudo ken and then put the tip of the thumb on the index knuckle. The thumb knuckle should be protruding upwards. It is used for striking soft targets, primarily the groin, inside of the thighs, and ribs.

Sanshiten Ken

Sanshiten Ken means "3 finger fist". The ring, middle, and index finger are squeezed together and the strike is delivered with the finger tips. Generally into soft tissue and hollows in the body.

Shishin Ken

Shishin ken means "finger needle" and is the term used to refer to any of the fingers striking, hooking, or grasping by itself.

Shikan Ken

Shikan ken is used to wedge the knuckles into narrow areas. From fudo ken extend all 4 knuckles forwards.

Shako Ken

Shako ken is used to claw, rake, and tear with the finger tips and nails.

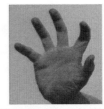

Happa Ken

Happa ken means "8 leaf strike" and is a clapping motion with both hands. Happa ken can be delivered 1 handed, although technically the name would change to "yonpa ken" (4 leaf) or

Shuki Ken

Shuki Ken is anytime the tip of the elbow is used to strike. This can be on a forehand, backhand, upwards, downwards, or rearwards movement.

Soki Ken

Soki ken is anytime the tip of the knee is used to deliver a strike. It can be while standing either attached or detached to any part of an opponent's body or can be delivered to a grounded opponent.

Sokugyaku Ken

Sokugyaku means "foot reversal" and is used to reference kicking with the ball of the foot. Kicking with this part of the foot can allow a strike to be pushed into the target in a thrusting motion. It is important to pull the toes back to expose the hard part just below them so that the toes aren't broken.

Sokuyaku Ken

Sokuyaku Ken means is striking with the heel.

Kikaku Ken

Kikaku ken means "demon horn strike" and refers to a head butt. The top part of the skull above the hairline is used to deliver a strike to the more fragile part of an opponent's head and face.

Ki Ken

Ki ken means "spirit fist." It refers not only to being able to intimidate someone or make them afraid of you with your own personal energy but also how you carry yourself regularly. With practice even a confident person can appear unconfident or vice-versa.

Tai Ken

Tai ken means "body fist" and refers to any motion of slamming the body into an opponent. This can be done against a standing opponent or a grounded opponent. It can also refer to the use of body weight to control someone on the ground.

7th Kyu

Introduction

In the nana (7th) kyu material students will learn how the kame and 16 jewels work together to make kata (forms). The sanshin no kata is the fundamental set of daken tai jutsu kata (striking methods) and teach the 8 directions of movement, how to block, kick, and strike with the hands.

Kanji

The kanji at 7th kyu allows for the structure of basic martial concepts. The characters in Japanese are Po 法, Do 道, and Jutsu 術. In order they translate as *Law*, *Way*, and *Art*. These 3 words, along with the 8th kyu characters, begin to form how martial arts are named. Lets precede each of these with Nin to illustrate. Ninpo would become the Laws of Stealth. This indicates a martial arts that's going to emphasize stealth and the clandestine concepts as it's root. Ninjutsu then becomes the Art of Stealth and alludes to the physical techniques to achieve Ninpo. Nindo would mean The Way of Stealth but this actually isn't allowed in Japanese language. Do (Way) indicates a more spiritual endeavor. Chado for example is the Way of Tea and emphasises the meditative process in the tea ceremony. There is no spiritual endeavor of covert activities however. They are only a survival tool. So then we turn to the 8th kyu work Bu. These two combined become Budo and indicate the character or life skills building portion of martial arts training.

Technique #1. Oten Ryote

1. Oten Ryote means 2-handed cartwheel.
2. To begin spread the feet apart and extend the hands overhead. (fig. 1)
3. Look to the spot where your hands will make contact with the ground and begin "wheeling" in that direction. If travelling to the right the right hand will touch the ground first. Let the second hand make contact with the ground and lift the legs off the ground, far leg first. Maintain a Star shape in the body while inverted (fig. 2)
4. Land the feet first and resume an upright posture bringing the hands off the ground. (fig. 3)
5. Students often have difficulty "throwing themselves" into the cartwheel but the momentum will help.

Technique #2. Chi no Kata

1. Chi no Kata is the "earth pattern".
2. To begin both the tori and uke are in ichimonji no kamae with their left feet and hands forwards.
3. The uke steps forwards on the right and attempts to deliver a front punch to the tori's face.
4. The tori shuffle steps straight back so that they are still in left ichimonji. They use the left hand to deliver a high block to the inside of the uke's right forearm. (fig.1)
5. Next the tori steps forwards on the right to ihen no kamae and delivers a boshi ken to the neck of the uke. (fig.2)

Technique #3. Sui no Kata

1. Sui no kata is the "water form" and should be performed with a feeling of flowing backwards and then crashing in from an angle.

2. From both opponents in shizen no kamae the uke steps forwards and attempts a high punch with the right hand to the tori's face.
3. The tori steps rearwards and to the right on a 45 degree angle and uses doko no kamae to perform a high block to the inside of the uke's right forearm.
4. The tori performs a sliding footswitch by sliding their left foot back to the right and then stepping forwards with the right foot.
5. Lastly the tori delivers an omote shuto to the left side of the uke's neck with their right hand. The strike is delivered into horizontally into the neck.

Technique #4. Ka no Kata

1. Ka no Kata is the "fire pattern".
2. To begin both the tori and uke are in ichimonji no kamae with their left feet and hands forwards.
3. The uke steps forwards on the right and attempts to deliver a front punch to the tori's face.
4. The tori shuffle steps straight back and to the right on an angle so that they are still in left ichimonji. They use the left hand to deliver a high block to the inside of the uke's right forearm. (fig.1)
5. Next the tori steps forwards on the right to jumonji no kamae and delivers an ura shuto ken to the right side of the neck of the uke. (fig.2)

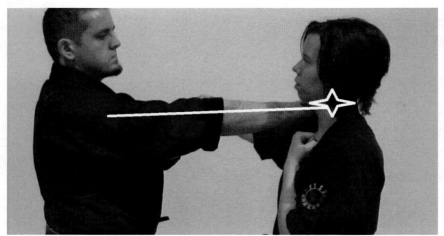

Technique #5. Fu no Kata

1. Fu no Kata is the "air pattern".
2. To begin both the tori and uke are in shizen no kamae.
3. The uke kicks forwards with the right foot attempting to deliver a kick to the tori's stomach.
4. The tori shuffle steps straight sideways to their right. They use the left hand to deliver a low block to the inside of the uke's right leg. (fig.1)
5. Next the tori steps forwards on the right and delivers a boshi ken to the hip of the uke. (fig.2)

Technique #6. Ku no Kata

1. Fu no Kata is the "void pattern".
2. To begin both the tori and uke are in shizen no kamae.
3. The uke kicks forwards with the right foot attempting to deliver a kick to the tori's stomach.
4. The tori shuffle steps straight sideways to their right. They use the left hand to catch the uke's right leg by inverting their hand to the inside. (fig.1)
5. Next the tori delivers a kick with their right foot to the inside of the uke's right leg. (fig.2)

6th Kyu

Introduction

The 6th kyu exam is intended to begin to begin teaching students how to counter attack using the attackers energy against them. This is referred to as Gyaku Waza and means Reversal Skill. It also introduces Tai Hodoki-Body Escapes.

Kanji

The kanji for 6th kyu are 気 "ki", 空 "kara/ku", 士 "shi", and 鳳 "hou". Respectively they mean "energy", "empty", "enlightened", and "phoenix". These 3 kanji taught at the green belt level are intended to help students begin to read more complex sentences and concepts.

Technique #1. Omote Gyaku

1. Omote gyaku is an outside wrist lock. It begins by the uke grabbing the tori's collar.
2. The tori steps back on the side being grabbed and hooks the same hand over the uke's thumb so that their fingers wrap around into the uke's palm and their palm is across the uke's knuckles. The support hand goes underneath the uke's hand and secures the tori's own shirt.
3. Next the tori pulls the uke's hand off the shirt as they pull their shirt towards their own chest with the support hand.
4. Next both hands come together to secure a grip around the uke's hand and twist to the outside.
5. The tori must remain in balance as the uke's balance is broken rearwards.

Technique #2. Omote Gyaku no Tsuki

1. Omote gyaku no tsuki is an outside wrist lock after blocking an incoming punch. It begins by the uke grabbing the tori's collar with their right hand and punching with their left.
2. The tori steps back on the side being grabbed and hooks the same hand over the uke's thumb so that their fingers wrap around into the uke's palm and their palm is across the uke's knuckles. The support hand performs a high block to the inside of the incoming arm.
3. Next the tori performs omote gyaku as before.

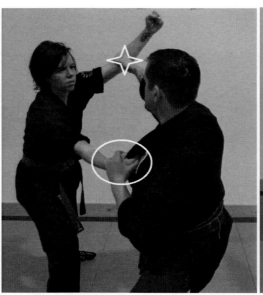 

Technique #3. Ura Gyaku

1. Ura gyaku means "inside reversal" or "inside wrist lock"
2. From a lapel grab the tori takes their far hand and reaches up and over the uke's grabbing hand. They secure their grip fingers over the pinky and thumb over the thumb. The support hand goes underneath the uke's hand and grabs the tori's own clothes. (fig.1)
3. The tori steps back and drops their weight and their elbow to pull the uke's grip off their clothes. To better facilitate the escape the support hand pulls the clothes towards the chest out of the uke's grip.
4. Next twist the uke's wrist to the inside.
5. From here the support hand adopts a grip beside the dominant hand and together continue to twist to the inside position until the uke bends over at the waist and falls forwards. (fig.2&3)

Technique # 4. Pyramid body escape

1. The first Tai Hodoki technique teaches students how to create space to be able to move when an attackers wrapped their body. All the tai hodoki techniques start from a rear "bear hug" with the attackers arms around the elbows of the tori.
2. From the grab the tori drops their posture from their knees slightly and pushes their hands downwards at a 45degree angle. This should open space between the tori's arms and their own body. It's important to note here that the movement isn't upwards against the uke's resistance.
3. The tori drops down and once the uke's arms are half way up their upper arm the lift up and grasp the uke's forearms or wrists so that they can't adjust their grip. From here finishing moves can be applied.

Technique #5. Breast stroke body escape

1. This waza starts the same as before but instead of the tori raising their hands up and their body down once they've created space they push both their hands out from their center line and then open up in a circular fashion, as though they were making a breast stroke in water.
2. Again once the uke's arms slide up the upper arm moguri (dropping elevation) and grabbing can be used to finish the escape.

Technique # 6. Isometric tension body escape

1. The tori can use isometric tension to create the space to move in. Much like driving down on a 45 degree angle opens some space, the tori can instead bend their arms at the elbows and try to tough their elbows together behind them.
2. This opens the chest and loads tension through the upper body. It can be much more difficult for the uke to counter.

Technique # 7. Knuckle grind body escape

1. The knuckle grind attacks the back of the uke's hand to create pain and damage causing them to open their grip.
2. Fist the tori stabilizes their posture and balance. Next the use shikan ken to extend their knuckles on one hand and grab the uke's hands with the other. This creates counter pressure.
3. Lastly the tori oscillates the shikan ken into the back of the uke's hand damaging and hurting the tendons that attach to the fingers. Once the grip is open the tori can employ finishing techniques.

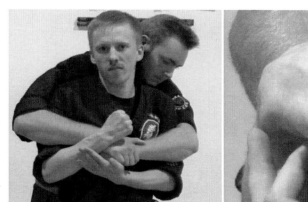
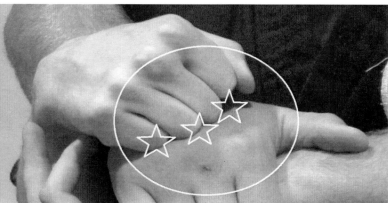

5 th Kyu

Introduction

Fifth (go) kyu introduces the student to the Daken Tai Jutsu forms (kata's) in the kihon happo. The first two covered are Ichimonji and Jumonji Kata. These two teach the student how to move forwards and backwards (shirabe) and circular (sabaki).

Kanji

The kanji for 5th kyu are  "ju", "go", "jo", "kan", and "sha". Respectively they mean "gentle", "hard", "place", "house" and "man who is employed as". They complete a student's ability to identify schools and system names and types.

Technique #1. Ichimonji no Kata

1. The uke and tori are facing each other, each in ichimonji no kamae with their left legs and arms forwards.
2. Uke steps forwards with the right foot and attempts to punch the tori in the face over top of their lead arm.
3. The tori shuffle steps rearwards slightly and performs a high block with their left hand to the inside of the uke's right arm. (fig.1)
4. Tori steps forwards with their right foot and performs a shuto strike with their right hand straight downwards onto the uke's collar bone.

Technique #2. Jumonji no Kata

1. Jumonji no Kata is the "# 10 pattern".
2. To begin both the tori and uke are in ichimonji no kamae with their left feet and hands forwards.
3. The uke steps forwards on the right and attempts to deliver a front punch to the tori's face.
4. The tori shuffle steps straight back and to the right on an angle and adopts jumonji no kamae. They use the left hand to deliver a high block to the inside of the uke's right forearm and then a boshi ken to the uke's right arm pit (fig.1).
5. The uke steps forwards on the left and attempts to deliver a front punch to the tori's face.
6. The tori shuffle steps straight back and to the left on an angle and adopts jumonji no kamae. They use the right hand to deliver a high block to the inside of the uke's left forearm (fig.2) and then a boshi ken to the uke's left arm pit (fig.3).

Technique #3. Moving the Bail of Rice

1. This is the first technique for te hodoki (hand escapes) and helps students learn the basic concepts of escapes.
2. To begin the attacker seizes both wrists (fig. 1).
3. Step to one direction on a forwards 45 degree angle and using the chest muscles push both hands forwards and up (fig.2)
4. Step on a forwards 45 degree to the opposite direction as the hands come over the opponents head and beside them. (fig. 4&5)
5. Imagine stepping forwards and lifting a bag or rice over the opponents head and putting it down beside them on the other side.

Technique #4. Opening Lotus

1. Opening lotus is a hand escape. Like the rest of the techniques in this rank it reinforces the transition between jumonji no kamae and kosei no kamae.
2. To begin the uke grabs both wrists of the tori. (fig. 1)
3. The tori uses their chest muscles to push their hands together and cross them. One of the tori's arms should cross the one of the uke's arms and the other the tori's own arm. (fig.2)
4. Next the tori rotates their wrists in as they push down on their own arm and the uke's. This creates a wedging action and counter pressure for the escape. (fig.3)
5. Finally the arm touching the uke's pushes down and the other arm pulls up to get the top wrist free. The tori finishes in kosei no kamae. (fig.4)

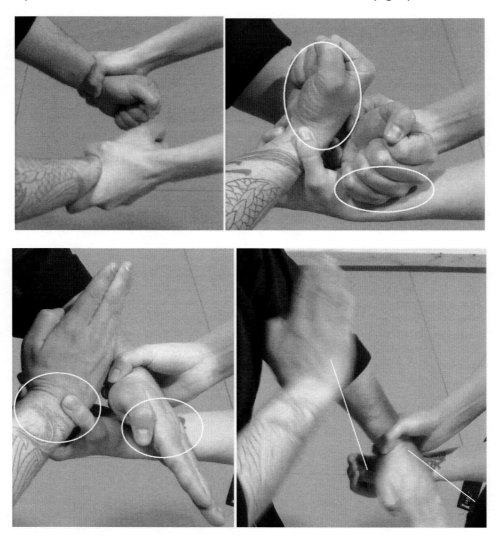

Technique #5. Prayer to Heaven

1. To many students Prayer to Heaven looks like it's completed with the arms and hands. Just like everything else in ninjutsu however there's much more going on, particularly in the legs and body.
2. From a double wrist grab the tori moves their torso closer to the their hands and drops their weight slightly.
3. From here the push up through the legs and body raising the hands. The hands are also pushed together to create tension and counter pressure.
4. Lastly the hands push up over the uke's head. The pressure should be back towards the uke, not straight up.

 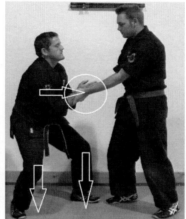 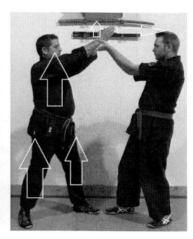

Technique # 6. Takagi Yoshin Omote Gyaku

1. From the double hand grab the tori seeks to push their hands together. If just the arms are used however the uke will keep this from happening. The tori can take a small step forwards and rotate their body to bring the hands together.
2. Once together, one hand goes under the other and grasps the uke's thumb.
3. The body is rotated back to starting position and the tori twists the uke's wrist to the outside, thereby completing omote gyaku but with an under grip instead of the usual over grip.

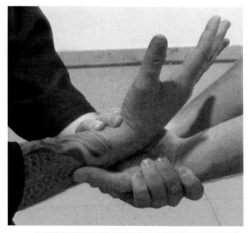

Technique # 7 Elbow Pressure

1. Elbow pressure can be used from a 2-handed grab. It's illustrated here with a single hand grab for clarity.
2. Simultaneously the tori steps towards the uke, rotates their wrist, and pushes their elbow towards the uke's elbow. This creates counter pressure and leverage and wedges the wrist out of the uke's grip.

4th kyu

Introduction

Fourth (yon) kyu is the last of the green belt ranks. By the time 4th kyu is complete students should be feeling confident to begin training in more complex skills. The final type of body movement is explored in Hicho Kata which teaches moguri (up and down movement). Footwork and walking skills are also taught (aruki or ashi waza).

Kanji

The kanji for 4th kyu are Koshi 腰, Hiza 膝, Hiji 肘, Ashi 足, Tai 体, Te 手. Respectively they mean "hips", "knee", "elbow", "foot", "body" and "hand".

Technique #1. Hicho Kata

1. Uke attacks with a right punch to the tori's stomach.
2. Tori steps back with their right leg and performs a low block with their left hand while at the same time adopting hicho no kamae (left leg up).
3. The tori lifts the uke's arm slightly and kicks up into the armpit with their toes.
4. The tori lands their foot back on the ground and does and ura shuto with their right hand to the right side of the uke's neck.

Technique #2. Neko Aruki

1. Neko aruki means "cat walking" and is designed not only to keep the foot protected while walking either barefoot or in minimal footwear but also to teach students the while moving the ball of the foot rather than the heel is used.
2. To perform the Cat Walk land on the ball of the foot just behind the toes instead of the heel. (fig. 1)
3. Neko Aruki can be performed slowly for stealth, regular speed for fighting, or while running for escape and evasion.

Technique #3. Shinobi Aruki

1. Shinobi Aruki means "stealth walk(ing)".
2. It is performed by first turning sideways and dropping low to present a small profile to any target.
3. Next the rear leg crosses in front of the lead shin and lands on the ball of the foot.

4. Slowly transfer the weight of the body onto the now-front foot. Once enough weight is transferred lift the now-rear foot and place it on the ground using the ball of the foot approximately shoulder width apart.
5. Repeat.

Technique #4. Kou Aruki

1. Kou Aruki is the "crane walk". It is used for walking though water, snow, or deep grass.
2. When performing kou aruki the goal is to maintain balance and lift the feet high by focusing on lifting the knee high.
3. Each step isn't very far but rather only moves the person a few inches at a time.
4. Be sure to that the ball of the foot is the first thing to land and last thing to leave the ground.

Technique #5. Hirai Aruki

1. Hirai Aruki is the "sweeping walk". It is used for walking moving debris out of the way while stealth walking.
2. While maintaining balance use the outside ridge of the foot to move any debris that might make sound or injure the foot out of the way to the outside. Only move it as much as necessary. Sometimes the debris may be lifted and the foot placed underneath it in order to limit any tracks left behind.

Technique #6. Hajai Aruki

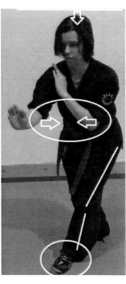

1. Hajai Aruki is "fast walking". It is used when a need arises to cover a distance quickly and still stay as quiet and as invisible as possible. It also works very well with modern footwear that has thick heavy soles.
2. While moving forwards crouch down as low as possible and pull both elbows into the chest in order to create a small profile.
3. Roll the feet from the outside of the heel to the inside of the big toe with every step.
4. Use the bent knees to absorb as much sound as possible.

5. The steps are kept small by almost touching the heel of the travelling foot to the toes of the posted foot.

Technique #7. Ushiro Aruki

1. Ushiro aruki is rearwards stepping. Although it's practiced many steps in a row, realistically a person would only make 1 or 2 steps rearwards either while sneaking or in a fight.
2. To begin from shizen no kamae lift the heel of one foot until only the toes are touching the ground. Slide that foot rearwards. (fig.1)
3. Repeat on the other side.

3rd kyu

Introduction

San kyu (3rd kyu) is a very important rank that few students reach. The change in belt colour from green to brown denotes maturity and skill but also responsibility. Students at this level should be able to begin to self manage and work through technical problems without as close supervision. The technical material covers ground fighting (ne waza) and the grappling techniques of the kihon happo.

Kanji

The kanji at this rank are very important in martial arts and represent growth from martial arts being purely extrinsic and external to a more internal process. The 7 Japanese words for 3rd kyu are commonly referred to as the "virtues of bushido" and represent the idea that martial arts are equally about dealing with internal conflict as much as they are about external conflict.

1. The kanji are Rei 礼, Makoto 誠, Jin 仁, Yuki 勇氣, Gi 義, Meiyo 名誉, Chugi 忠義. In order they mean Respect, Honesty, Kindness, Courage, Integrity, Honour, and Loyalty.

Technique #1. Hiza Dori

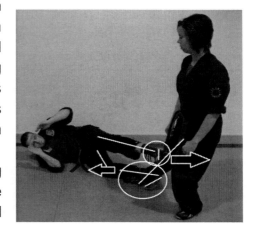

1. The term knee bar is used anytime an opponent's knee is made to lock out through hyper extending it. The straight leg is then used as a lever to shift the hips thereby manipulating balance. In this program this technique is specifically used when the tori finds themselves on the ground and the uke standing over them at their feet.
2. To begin the tori rolls onto 1 side. Using whatever foot corresponds with the side they're lying on the hook the uke's heel from behind with the toes.
3. Using the foot that's in the air the tori makes contact just below the uke's knee and pushes the knee back up.
4. Once the knee is locked the leg will lever the uke's hips knocking them down.

Technique #2. Ashi Waru

1. The leg chop is used when the tori is on the ground and the uke is standing over them but the two are perpendicular to each other.
2. The tori faces away from the uke on their side and puts their low foot over the top of the uke's foot.
3. Using the foot in the air they chop with a leg curl into the back of the uke's knee pushing it forwards and down.

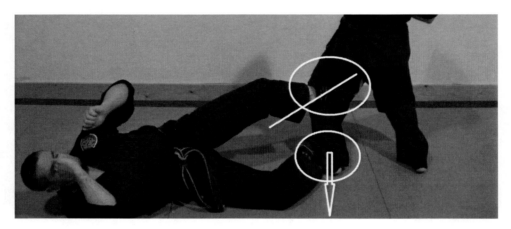

Technique #3. Upa

1. The bridge is one of the most important ground fighting techniques (ne waza). Many bullies and street thugs will use a tackle to knock someone down and then sit on their core and strike them in the head and face. This is very dangerous for the person on their back.
2. From the mount (tori lying on their back with uke straddling their chest/hips) the tori begins by holding down one of the uke's arms and trapping the corresponding foot.
3. Next the tori uses the balls of their feet to lift their hips off the ground as high as they can.
4. Lastly the tori pivots off one shoulder and rotates up and over it on a 45 degree angle.

  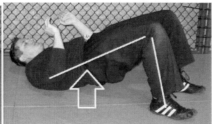

Technique #4. Hasami Bare

1. The scissor sweep is performed when the uke is in the tori's guard and the tori wishes to reverse positions. The guard position is with the tori lying on their back and the uke kneeling (seiza) between their legs. From here the tori can wrap the uke with their arms and legs to hold them down so that the uke can't strike them.
2. To begin the scissor sweep the tori first rolls onto 1 side (while still under the uke). This is done by pushing off the ground with 1 foot and rolling onto a hip. Now the tori will have 1 leg flat to the ground. The opposite knee pushes up into the uke's floating ribs.
3. The tori finishes by scissoring their legs across each other THROUGH the uke's core and rolling.
4. The tori should stay with the uke as the uke falls to the side and finishes on the uke's mount.

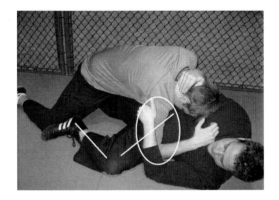
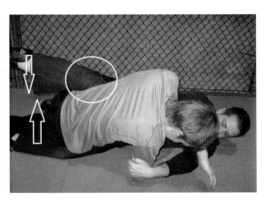

Technique #5. Hasami Geri

1. The scissor kick technique is done to reverse an attacker on Rear Mount. The rear mount position is when the tori finds themselves face down on the ground with the uke straddled across their hips on their back.
2. It is very important when performing the scissor kick to NOT LIFT THE HIPS. An experienced (or lucky) attacker can slip their feet underneath the tori making it nearly impossible to escape.
3. With the hips still flat on the ground the tori crosses their legs in a large scissoring motion. Start with the feet and let the scissor travel up the legs into the hips. This will rotate the hips under the uke.

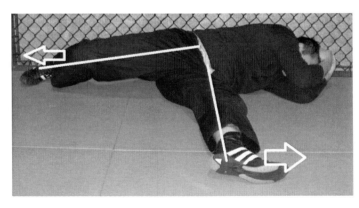

4. When the hips rotate 1 of 2 things might happen. The first is the uke will fall off the tori. The second thing that might occur is the uke stays on top but the tori rotates under them. This will put the uke on the mount. From here the tori can bridge to escape.

Technique #6, Ebi

1. The tori lifts their hips to clear your body off the ground, push off the ground with the balls of the feet and simultaneously shoot hips back and reach for the feet.

2. When an opponent is in your guard Shrimping can be used to create space. After creating space insert a shin and knee to create the corner and keep the subject away from you.

3. Once you create space you can adopt the Back Ground Fight Position and engage with kicks.

Technique #7 Ura Ebi

1. In certain situations you can't move the other person. In these situations a transition method

known as "reverse shrimp" properly called in Japanese "ura ebi" is utilized. The concept of ura ebi escape can be utilized from any position where the assailant is on top and you are supine.
2. Where the ebi pushes the tori using the legs, ura ebi pulls the tori using the legs. When done against an uke the arms can be used to assist.
3. To utilize the Back Door Escape from a failed bridge maintain hip elevation and inserting one arm below the opponents' inner thigh.
4. Use the inserted arm to create pressure over your head as hips fall back into the space and legs pull you out from under the opponent. Turn to face your adversary and adopt the Back Ground Fight Position.

Technique #8 Yoko Ebi

1. Yoko Ebit means side shrimp and is used much the same way as the regular Ebi except that the opponent is beside the tori.
2. To perform the technique the tori lays on their side facing the uke and uses their top elbow and knee to block a mount attempt.
3. Using the foot that's laying on the ground the tori digs the ball of their foot into the ground and lifts their hips slightly.
4. Using their foot and leg they push their hips back away from the uke.

Technique #9 Kame

1. The term kame means "turtle" in English. It is used when the tori finds themselves on the ground face down with the uke either standing over them or behind them.
2. From a kneeling position the tori shifts their hips back onto their heels and wraps both hands over the back of their head and neck. The elbows touch the knees to stop an opponent from getting their legs around the tori's waist.
3. This posture cannot be hold long but rather is used as a temporary transition to momentarily protect against chokes and strikes to the back of the head.

Technique #10. San Kaku

1. San Kaku means "pyramid". It is used to move out of the kame position and facilitate a back door escape.
2. It is important when performing the pyramid that the tori first widens their base by spreading their feet and hands apart.
3. Next they extend their hips back by pushing up and back with their legs. It is crucial at this stage that the elbows stay on the ground.
4. Lastly the tori uses their arms to push their body rearwards to their feet.

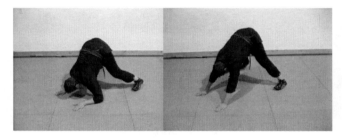

Technique #11. Oni Kudaki

1. Oni Kudaki means "killing the demon." It is a shoulder lock to manipulate an opponent's balance to the rear an knock them down.
2. From an incoming punch the tori performs jumonji no kamae and lets the punch pass between their hands. They step to the uke's inside and allows their arms to spread apart so that one hand is across the inside of the uke's wrist and the other arm is behind their upper arm. (fig.1)
3. The tori rotates their hips away from the uke and pulls their elbow down to bend the uke's arm. Continue to rotate until the hands come together. (fig. 2&3)
4. To finish the uke lifts up on the uke's elbow and down on their hand to break their balance to the rear.

2nd kyu

Introduction

The 2nd (ni) kyu is a very difficult level because of the focus on throws and takedowns (nage waza).

Kanji

1. The kanji for 2nd kyu are 3 terms used to describe good body mechanics (tai jutsu). The terms are Shirabe 調, Moguri 潜, Sabaki 捌, Hei 兵, In 陰, Yo 陽, Kyo 強, Jyaku 弱

. The term shirabe means to investigate or enter, moguri has to do with changing body elevation, and sabaki means to turn or rotate. Hei means soldier. In-Yo is the Japanese equivalent of Yin-Yang and means Dark-Light. Kyo translates to strong and Jyaku weak.

Technique #1. Musha Dori

1. Musha Dori means "capturing the warrior" and it is primarily used to entangle an opponent's weapon arm with the support arm, thereby leaving the tori's weapon arm free to engage.
2. To begin the uke grabs the tori's shoulder. The tori steps slightly to the uke's inside position and raises their arm up between them and the uke. (fig. 1)
3. Next the tori inverts their hand and bends their elbow so that their arm collapses over the uke's. The uke's elbow should be pinched by the tori's. (fig.2)
4. The tori then drops their posture and pushes the uke's elbow straight down to the ground. (fig.3)
5. To finish the tori lifts the uke's elbow using their legs. The uke's posture is broken to the rear while the tori is still standing straight. (fig. 4)

Technique #2. Ganseki Nage

1. Ganseki nage begins with both opponents facing each other in shizen no kamae. The tori begins by cross stepping forwards and placing their right foot between the uke's feet. Their right arm inserts under the uke's left arm and hooks up and over the uke's shoulder as they turn 180 degrees to face the same direction as the uke.
2. If step 1 is performed properly the tori will be standing in front of the uke and slightly off to one side with their right leg in front of the uke's left leg and their right arm under the uke's left arm and capturing the uke's shoulder.
3. From here the tori slides their right leg straight back and their right arm forwards thereby tripping the uke forwards.

Technique #3. Ganseki Nage Henka (yoko)

1. The sideways variation on ganseki nage should come out of uke's resistance. The uke either plants 1 leg forwards of the other one rearwards to defend ganseki nage.
2. From this position the tori changes the direction of force from forwards (where the uke has established a defense) to sideways. The tori does this by taking a big step sideways across the uke's center line.
3. As an option the tori may step across the center line and behind the opposite foot and hook it from the inside.
4. From here the tori shifts their weight to the same side that they stepped taking the uke off balance.

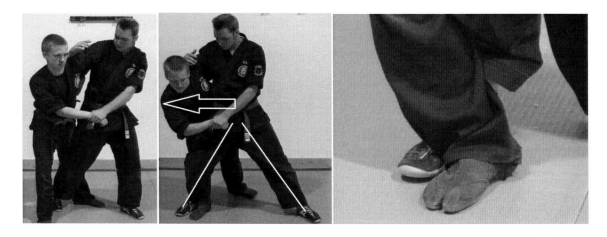

Technique #4. Ganseki Goshi

1. Ganseki goshi starts out the same as ganseki nage but instead of using a trip the tori juts their hip across the uke's and lifts them onto it using sabaki (rotation).
2. If the tori is taller than the uke they have to use their knees to ensure their center of mass is lower than the uke's.

Technique #5. Harai Goshi

1. Harai Goshi uses a rear leg lift to block an uke's jump defense.
2. From the same entry as ganseki goshi the tori begins to lift the uke onto their hip.
3. The tori takes the leg that's inside the uke's center line, lifts it, and kicks backwards across the uke's waist. The kick should be back and up lifting the uke's center of mass.

Technique #6. Seoi Nage

1. To begin Seo Nage enter the same as Ganseki Nage. Instead of capturing the arm however drop the hand low and grab the uke's body at their hips.
2. Once the tori is in position they insert their hips across the uke's center line and using the legs lift up.
3. Using the arms pull the uke around the hips.

 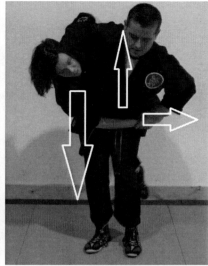

Technique #7. O'Soto Gari

1. To begin o'soto gari both opponents are facing each other in shizen no kamae. The tori grabs the uke's right wrist with their left hand and extends it outwards. The tori takes a step forwards with their left foot and stands beside the uke, the uke's arm in front of their chest.
2. The tori inserts their right foot behind the uke's right foot and grabs the uke's left shoulder with their right hand.
3. Next the tori pushes their hand forwards and foot rearwards thereby tripping the uke down to the ground backwards.

Technique #8. O'Soto Nage

1. O'Soto Nage begins the same as o'soto gari.
2. Instead of keeping space for the trip however, the tori juts their hip behind and below the uke's. If the tori is taller than the uke they must use moguri to get their center of mass lower than the uke's.
3. From this position the tori extends their hips up and back into the tori while simultaneously pushing forwards with their upper attachment.
4. Be very careful while training this technique. Often uke's will invert rearwards and hit the back of their heads on the ground.

Technique #9. Tomoe Nage

1. Tomoe Nage is a sutemi waza (sacrifice throw) whereby the tori throws the uke to the ground by throwing themselves to the ground.
2. To begin both opponents are facing each other in shizen no kamae. The tori grabs both lapels of the uke's gi.
3. The tori begins to sit backwards and when their body makes contact with the ground they put 1 foot across the hips of the uke.
4. While continuing their rearwards momentum the tori extends their leg and pulls the uke up and over them

Technique #10. Temakura

1. Temakura means "hand pillow." It is one of the few techniques that Takamatsu sensei demonstrated on film.
2. Although it can be performed on a punching opponent it is easiest to learn it from a front grab.
3. From the uke grasping the tori's collar, the tori rotates their hips and reaches across their center line and under the uke's grabbing arm with their far hand while their closest hand grabs the uke's knuckles and holds it in place.
4. Next the tori traps the uke's arm by flexing their arm and trapping the uke's arm in the crook of the elbow. The tori grabs the back of their own head with the trapping hand.
5. The foot that corresponds with the trapping arm applies a hidden kick to the uke's shin which corresponds with the trapped arm. The tori throws themselves backwards to the ground while twisting slightly towards the trapping side performing a sutemi waza.
6. When applied properly this will lock the uke's elbow and use leverage to force them to the ground with the tori.

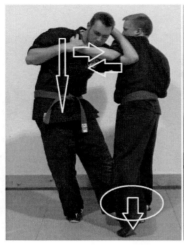

Technique #11. Sui Ryu

1. Sui ryu is very similar to tomoe nage. Most of the mechanics are the same.
2. The distinguishing difference between sui ryu and tomoe nage is that instead of the tori's foot pushing into the waist of the uke, it traps the inside of the uke's thigh. Notice that this is a trap and lift *AND NOT* a groin kick.

Technique #12. Yoko Nagare Henka

1. To begin yoko nagare henka both opponents begin facing each other in shizen no kamae and the tori grabs the lapels of the uke with both hands. (fig.1)

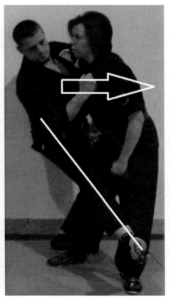

2. The tori then glides forwards to the uke's right side and turns sideways to face the uke.
3. The tori extends the right leg across both of the uke's shins and completes a side fall onto their right buttock pulling the uke down by the lapels and tripping them over the back of their extended right leg. The tori should use their eyes to look where they want the uke to land to ensure a nice side fall. (fig.2&3)

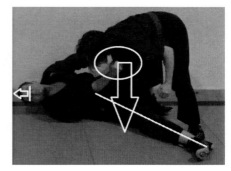

Technique #13. Yoko Nagare Henka 2

1. For the second yoko nagare henka instead of turning away from the uke and extending a leg the tori turns into the uke and collapses it.
2. From the starting position the tori takes their right foot and places it on the uke's right hip. Next they push their shin into the uke's chest.
3. The tori falls backwards as they pull the uke towards them with their hands and away from them with their shin. As the tori falls they twist to the right.
4. When executed properly the uke will fall perpendicular to the tori. The shin can be used to flip the uke up and over to their back.

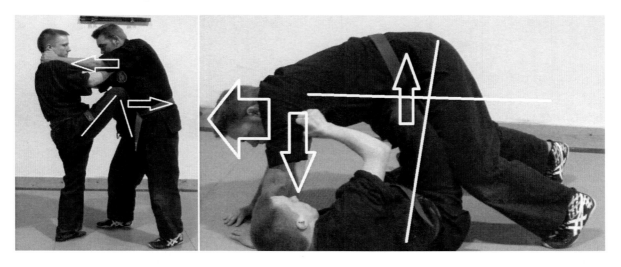

Technique #14. Yoko Nagare Henka 3 (ushiro)

1. The third variation on the sideways throw is nearly identical to the first but it's done to throw the uke rearwards.
2. From the start position the tori lifts up one arm of the uke and ducks their head under it. Wrap the uke's torso with both arms while standing perpendicular to them.
3. Extend one leg straight out behind the uke and fall to that side. The tori should be sure to look over that shoulder as they fall as to make sure their skull doesn't get crushed between the uke and the ground on landing.
4. Just before impact the tori lets their grip go and performs yoko ukemi.

Technique #15. Kata Garuma

1. Kata Garuma means "shoulder wheel throw" and is known in wrestling as a "fireman's carry throw."
2. Like all throws it can be performed from any attack but for the sake of description it'll be described from defending an incoming punch.
3. The tori receives the punch and grasps a wrist.
4. Next the tori uses moguri to lower and enter their free hand between the uke's legs and wraps the leg that corresponds with the trapped hand.

5. When the tori stands back up they will have the uke in a "fireman's carry," horizontal across their shoulders.
6. The tori tilts their shoulders towards the direction the uke is facing to complete the throw. There is a kneeling henka.

Technique #16. Morote Gari

1. The double leg takedown is a technique from freestyle wrestling.
2. To begin the tori and uke face each other in shizen no kamae.
3. The tori drops their posture using their legs. Fix the eyes on a high point behind the uke to keep the back straight. Step forwards on a slight angle just beside the uke. (fig. 1-2)
4. The tori grabs the backs of both of the uke's knees and presses their head against the uke's side.
5. While continuing to push against the uke's side with the side of their head the tori pulls the uke's knees out from under them. (fig.3)

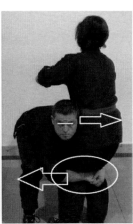

Technique #17. O'Gyaku Kata

1. This kata along with sprawling and jaw control teaches students how to defend themselves against throws.
2. To begin the uke grabs the tori's lapels and attempts seo nage.
3. The uke steps back with their inside foot while simultaneously pushing against the small of the uke's back/upper hips with the corresponding hand and trapping the uke's hand with their outside hand.

4. Next the tori leaps over the uke's legs and lands in front of the uke. The tori strikes the uke with a fudo ken and then drops their elbow down between the uke's hands breaking the grip on their gi.
5. The tori finishes by applying ganseki nage.

Technique #18. Sprawl

1. A sprawl is used to defend against the double leg takedown in 5th kyu.
2. As the uke shoots in for the tackle the tori puts their hands together and makes a triangle shape with the forearms.
3. They shoot their hips rearwards as they push the forearm triangle into the uke's shoulder on 1 side of their head.

Technique #19. Jaw Control

1. Sometimes when sprawling the attacker can still manage to grab 1 leg. When this happens the jaw control technique is used.
2. From a 1 leg grab the tori slides their hand down the outside of the grabbed leg until their forearm is in between the attackers head and their leg. (fig.1)
3. Next they curl their arm until their forearm is across the uke's face and they can get their hands together in a grip. (fig.2)
4. Using the legs lift up and rotate the body thereby rotating the uke's jaw and neck affecting their balance. (fig.3)

  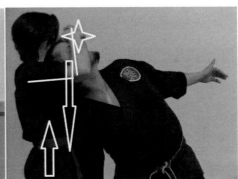

1st kyu

Introduction

The brown belt ranks gradually focus on techniques that are more challenging in terms of body control and memorization. The ichi kyu level focus' on weapon skills (buki waza) and prepares a student (deshi) for black belt.

Kanji

The 1st kyu kanji's are Chi 地, Sui 水, Ka 火, Fu 風, Ken 拳, Ken 剣, Ai 合, and Hodoki 解. In order they mean earth, water, fire, air, fist, sword, harmony, and escape.

Technique #1. Kuji Kiri

1. Kuji Kiri means "9 way cutting" and is the basic kenjutsu (sword) and tanto jutsu (knife) training kata (form). There are 9 cuts to the pattern that, when completed, for and asterix.
2. When scoring the performance of the kata timing between body movement and impact with the tip of the blade across the tori's center line is what's measured and scored.
3. Whenever a cut starts on the right the right foot should be forwards and vice versa for the left side.
4. Follow the photo sequence to complete the kata.

Technique #2. Overhead blocks

1. The term "block" is not quit accurate when describing the overhead interceptions in kenjutsu. The overhead blocks are more of a deflection. They can be demonstrated in either order.
2. To perform the overhead the uke feeds angle #1, men kiri. The tori side steps slightly to either the right or the left and the sword is raised overhead on a 45 degree angle over their head. Use the side of the blade to block.
3. Repeat on the other side.

Technique #3. Press blocks

1. The press blocks are performed when the uke attacks on angles 2, 3, 6, &7.
2. The tori steps forwards into the incoming strike with whichever foot is opposite the side being attacked. For angles 2 & 3 the sword is held close to the body tip up. For angles 6 & 7 tip down.
3. Ensure to hold the tsuka (handle) close to the body to use the core to absorb the impact of the strike.

Technique #4. Slap Parry

1. The slap parry is performed when the uke attacks on angle #9, skeeti (thrust).
2. When the thrust is incoming the tori side steps slightly moving out of the way of the stab.
3. The tori's sword raises higher than the uke's and slaps down on top of it using the side of the blade to knock the uke's sword down. Proper wrist alignment ensures the tori's grip and adds energy to the parry.

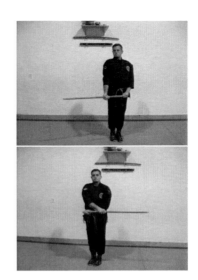

Technique #5. Hanbo Jutsu Uchi Waza Kata

1. Uchi waza means striking skill. This kata is a basic kata that incorporates handwork, footwork, and body mechanics to use a hanbo (1/2 or 3' staff) properly.
2. Steps 1-4 incorporate v-stepping forwards and backwards, the striking hand matches the forward foot, and both hands are palm down.
3. Steps 5-8 also incorporate the v-step but this time the striking hand matches the rearwards foot.
4. Steps 9-10 utilize a rearwards c-step with a strike to the head.
5. Strikes 11-12 are performed with a c-step but with a forwards thrust.
6. Strikes 13-14 flow from gedan no kamae (low posture) and the tori performs ahi bare (foot sweep).
7. Steps 15-16 are called tento uchi (striking on top of the head) and come straight down on angle 1.
8. Strikes 17-18 are called age uchi (raising strike) and the tip of the hanbo raises on angle 8 under the targets chin.
9. Lastly strikes 19 & 20 incorporate an overhead block with a flow to a conventional grip and a strike to the temple.

Technique #6. Hanbo Jutsu Oni Kudaki

1. Oni kudaki is a shoulder lock.
2. From an incoming punch the tori moves to the inside position and catches the uke's wrist with the mirror side hand. They simultaneously strike the uke's ribs with the hanbo.
3. Next the tori thrusts the hanbo forwards under the uke's arm and flips it up over the uke's arm.
4. A tessen ken (fan strike) is used to strike the uke in the face. The tip of the hanbo is inserted under the uke's chin and the tori pulls down on the uke's elbow using the hanbo as leverage.

Technique #7. Hanbo Jutsu tsuki iri

1. Tsuki iri is an arm bar using a hanbo. The technique starts from an incoming punch from the uke. The tori steps to the outside position and catches their wrist with their mirror side hand and strikes the uke's torso.
2. The tori turns towards the uke and performs jumonji no kamae crossing their wrists and the hanbo ovr the uke's elbow. The tip of the hanbo should put pressure into the uke's hips.
3. The tori walks forwards and applies pressure down to take down the uke.

Technique #8. Hanbo Jutsu Kocho Dori

1. Kocho dori means "capture the butterfly" and is an armbar applied from under the uke's arm. It is performed from an incoming punch.
2. The tori moves to the inside position and strikes upwards into the uke's arm with the hanbo in the mirror-side hand.

3. Next they flip the hanbo over the elbow and pulls the uke's wrist up onto their shoulder. The tori grasps the other end of the hanbo with their free hand and applies pressure just above the elbow.
4. The tori walks backwards and uses a j-stroke hand motion to finish the arm bar.

Technique #9. Hanbo Jutsu Ganseki Nage

1. From and incoming punch the tori steps to the inside and strikes the uke in the ribs with the tip of the hanbo.
2. Next they raise the tip of the hanbo into the uke's arm pit and steps forwards and c-steps tripping the uke to finish the throw.

Technique #10. Rouko Shako Bo Uchi Waza Kata

1. This 20 step kata follows the same pattern as the hanbo jutsu kata but is performed with a 6' staff instead of a 3' staff.

Technique #11. Bo Furi

1. Bo Furi is a fundamental flailing (spinning) technique in which the tori alternates which end of the weapon is exposed but utilizing a double hand switch to their side and striking upwards on angles 6,7,or 8.

Technique #11. Hachi Jin no Muashi

1. Hachi Jin no muashi is a figure 8 spin where the tori spins the staff upwards using a conventional grip and applies every strike with the dominant hand end of the staff.

Technique #12. Ura Hachi Jin no Muashi

1. Ura hachi jin no muashi is a figure 8 flail where the striking end of the staff raises up into the strikes instead of down.

Technique #13. Kuri Gaeshi

1. When performing kuri gaeshi the tori spins the staff diagonally behind their back and up over their shoulders.

Technique #14. Shuriken Jutsu Nage Waza

1. There are 4 fundamental methods of throwing shuriken.
2. Method #1 the tori uses bobi no kamae to hold the stars. They reach back with their forwards hand palm up and rock to ichimonji no kamae releasing the star flat.
3. Method #2 the tori loads a star in the rear hand of doko no kamae. They step forwards with their rear foot and drop their hand down on a vertical line releasing the star.
4. Method #3 the tori stands in bobi no kamae with their dominant hand and foot rearwards. They load a star in the rear hand and step forwards to ihen no kamae releasing the star up into the target on a vertical line.
5. To perform method #4 the tori throws the star by loading it in their dominant hand at their side with their dominant hand and foot rearwards. They rotate their hips inwards and releases the star palm up in an omote shuto fashion.

Shodan

Introduction

The final test is Shodan. Students who pass this exam will be rewarded their black belt and black Bujin patch to display over their heart on their uniform. Contrary to popular misconception Shodan (black belt) does not indicate mastery of a martial art. The word Shodan translates to beginner level. This rank indicates that a student has learned enough basics to begin experimenting with their own ideas in how to put the concepts to use. There aren't any new techniques between 1st kyu and shodan but the minimum passing score is 90% instead of 80%, there are 10 new attacks in randori, and 10 new kanji.

Kanji

The kanji for the shodan test relate to the different level of teachers in Bujinkan rank structure. They are Sensei 先生, Shidoshi 指道者, Shihan 師範, Soke 宗家, Ryu 龍, Tora 虎, Take 竹, Zen 禅, Shugyo 修行, and Nagare 流. Sensei means teacher, shidoshi means guide and is the term awarded at 5th dan. A shihan is an expert and is the title awarded at 10th dan. The term soke refers to the grandmaster. Ryu means dragon, Tora is tiger, Take bamboo, Zen is a peaceful state or awareness, Shugyo means quest, and Nagare means flow.

Testing Forms

Student Test Form

Full Name: _____
Current Rank: NIL
Requested Rank: 9th kyu
Total Training Hours: _____

Taihenjutsu Ukemi Gata /9			R	L	Vision
Zenpo Ryoho					
Koho					
Sayu yoko zenpo					
Etiquette /2					
		Belt Tying			
		Opening/Closing			
Kamae /12					
Seiza		Ichimonji			
Fudoza		Doko			
Shizen		Hoko			
Hicho		Hira			
Bobi		Ihen			
Jumonji		Kosei			
Self Defense /9	DESCRIPTION		R	L	VISION
Mae tsuki 1					
Mae geri 1					
Lapel grab 1					
Kanji /2					
Nin					
Written Exam %					
Randori: 10 linear					
Total Score /34 = %					

Notes:

Overall: P / F   Signed: _____Date: _____

Student Test Form

Full Name: _____
Current Rank: 9th kyu
Requested Rank: 8th kyu
Total Training Hours: _____

Taihenjutsu Ukemi Gata /18	R	L	Vision
Zenpo Ryoho			
Koho			
Sayu yoko zenpo			
Zenpo Kaiten			
Koho Kaiten			
Yoko Kaiten			
Etiquette /2			
	Belt Tying		
	Opening/Closing		

Kamae /12			
Seiza		Ichimonji	
Fudoza		Doko	
Shizen		Hoko	
Hicho		Hira	
Bobi		Ihen	
Jumonji		Kosei	

16 Jewels /16			
Fudo		Boshi	
Koppo		Shuto	
Sanshiten		Shikan	
Shishin		Happa	
Shako		Soki	
Shuki		Sokuyaku	
Sokugyaku		Tai	
Kikaku		Ki	

Self Defense /21	DESCRIPTION	R	L	VISION
Mei Tsuki 1				
Mei Tsuki 2				
Mei Tsuki 3				
Mei Geri 1				
Mei Geri 2				
Lapel Grab 1				
Lapel Grab 2				

Kanji /6	
Nin, Bu, Jin	
Randori: 20 circle drill	
Total Score /75 = %	

Notes:

Overall: P / F   Signed: _____ Date: _____

Student Test Form

Full Name: _____

Current Rank: 8th kyu

Requested Rank: 7th kyu

Total Training Hours: _____

Taihenjutsu Ukemi Gata /18		R	L	Vision
Zenpo Ryoho				
Koho				
Sayu yoko zenpo				
Zenpo Kaiten				
Koho Kaiten				
Yoko Kaiten				

Etiquette /2			
	Belt Tying		
	Opening/Closing		

Kamae /12			
Seiza		Ichimonji	
Fudoza		Doko	
Shizen		Hoko	
Hicho		Hira	
Bobi		Ihen	
Jumonji		Kosei	

16 Jewels /16			
Fudo		Boshi	
Koppo		Shuto	
Sanshiten		Shikan	
Shishin		Happa	
Shako		Soki	
Shuki		Sokuyaku	
Sokugyaku		Tai	
Kikaku		Ki	

Sanshin no Kata /15		R	L	Vision
	Chi no kata			
	Sui no kata			
	Ka no kata			
	Fu no kata			
	Ku no kata			

Self Defense /27	DESCRIPTION	R	L	VISION
Mei Tsuki 1				
Mei Tsuki 2				

Mei Tsuki 3				
Mei Tsuki 4				
Mei Geri 1				
Mei Geri 2				
Lapel Grab 1				
Lapel Grab 2				
Te Hodoki 1				
Kanji /12				
Nin, Bu, Jin, Po, Do, Jutsu				
Randori: 30 circle drill random order				
Total Score /102 = %				

Notes:

Overall: P / F   Signed: _____   Date: _____

Student Test Form

Full Name: _____
Current Rank: 7th kyu
Requested Rank: 6th kyu
Total Training Hours: _____

Taihenjutsu Ukemi Gata /18		R	L	Vision
Zenpo Ryoho				
Koho				
Sayu yoko zenpo				
Zenpo Kaiten				
Koho Kaiten				
Yoko Kaiten				
Etiquette /2				
	Belt Tying			
	Opening/Closing			
Kamae /12				
Seiza		Ichimonji		
Fudoza		Doko		
Shizen		Hoko		
Hicho		Hira		
Bobi		Ihen		
Jumonji		Kosei		
16 Jewels /16				
Fudo		Boshi		
Koppo		Shuto		
Sanshiten		Shikan		
Shishin		Happa		
Shako		Soki		
Shuki		Sokuyaku		
Sokugyaku		Tai		
Kikaku		Ki		
Sanshin no Kata /15		R	L	Vision
	Chi no kata			
	Sui no kata			
	Ka no kata			
	Fu no kata			
	Ku no kata			
Kihon Happo /9		R	L	Vision
	Omote Gyaku			
	Ura Gyaku			

			R	L	Vision
	Omote no Tsuki				
Tai Hodoki /12			R	L	Vision
	Pyramid				
	Breast Stroke				
	Isometric Tension				
	Knuckle Grind				
Self Defense /36	DESCRIPTION		R	L	VISION
Mei Tsuki 1					
Mei Tsuki 2					
Mei Tsuki 3					
Mei Tsuki 4					
Mei Tsuki 5					
Mei Geri 1					
Mei Geri 2					
Lapel Grab 1					
Lapel Grab 2					
Te Hodoki 1					
Te Hodoki 2					
Tai Hodoki 1					
Green Belt Stress Test					
Kanji /20					
Nin, Bu, Jin, Po, Do, Jutsu, Ki, Kara, Hou, Shi					
Randori: 40 include weapons					
Total Score /140 = %					

Notes:

Overall: P / F   Signed: _____   Date: _____

Student Test Form

Full Name: _____
Current Rank: 6th kyu
Requested Rank: 5th kyu
Total Training Hours: _____

Taihenjutsu Ukemi Gata /18		R	L	Vision
Zenpo Ryoho				
Koho				
Sayu yoko zenpo				
Zenpo Kaiten				
Koho Kaiten				
Yoko Kaiten				
Etiquette /2				
		Belt Tying		
		Opening/Closing		
Kamae /12				
Seiza		Ichimonji		
Fudoza		Doko		
Shizen		Hoko		
Hicho		Hira		
Bobi		Ihen		
Jumonji		Kosei		
16 Jewels /16				
Fudo		Boshi		
Koppo		Shuto		
Sanshiten		Shikan		
Shishin		Happa		
Shako		Soki		
Shuki		Sokuyaku		
Sokugyaku		Tai		
Kikaku		Ki		
Sanshin no Kata /15		R	L	Vision
	Chi no kata			
	Sui no kata			
	Ka no kata			
	Fu no kata			
	Ku no kata			
Kihon Happo /15		R	L	Vision
	Omote Gyaku			
	Ura Gyaku			
	Omote no Tsuki			

			R	L	Vision
	Ichimonji Kata				
	Jumonji Kata				
Tai Hodoki /12			R	L	Vision
	Pyramid				
	Breast Stroke				
	Isometric Tension				
	Knuckle Grind				
Te Hodoki /15			R	L	Vision
	Opening Lotus				
	Prayer to Heaven				
	Elbow Pressure				
	Takagi Yoshin Omote Gyaku				
	Moving the Bail of Rice				
Self Defense /39	**DESCRIPTION**		R	L	**VISION**
Mei Tsuki 1					
Mei Tsuki 2					
Mei Tsuki 3					
Mei Tsuki 4					
Mei Tsuki 5					
Mei Geri 1					
Mei Geri 2					
Lapel Grab 1					
Lapel Grab 2					
Te Hodoki 1					
Te Hodoki 2					
Tai Hodoki 1					
Newaza Bridging					
Kanji /30					
Nin, Bu, Jin, Po, Do, Jutsu, Ki, Kara, Hou, Shi, Jo, Kan, Sha, Ju, Go					
Randori: 50 include weapons					
Total Score /174 = %					

Notes:

Overall: P / F   Signed: _____   Date: _____

Student Test Form

Full Name: _____
Current Rank: 5th kyu
Requested Rank: 4th kyu
Total Training Hours: _____

Taihenjutsu Ukemi Gata /18		R	L	Vision
Zenpo Ryoho				
Koho				
Sayu yoko zenpo				
Zenpo Kaiten				
Koho Kaiten				
Yoko Kaiten				
Etiquette /2				
		Belt Tying		
		Opening/Closing		
Kamae /12				
Seiza		Ichimonji		
Fudoza		Doko		
Shizen		Hoko		
Hicho		Hira		
Bobi		Ihen		
Jumonji		Kosei		
16 Jewels /16				
Fudo		Boshi		
Koppo		Shuto		
Sanshiten		Shikan		
Shishin		Happa		
Shako		Soki		
Shuki		Sokuyaku		
Sokugyaku		Tai		
Kikaku		Ki		
Sanshin no Kata /15		R	L	Vision
	Chi no kata			
	Sui no kata			
	Ka no kata			
	Fu no kata			
	Ku no kata			
Kihon Happo /18		R	L	Vision
	Omote Gyaku			

		R	L	Vision
	Ura Gyaku			
	Omote no Tsuki			
	Ichimonji Kata			
	Jumonji Kata			
	Hicho Kata			
Tai Hodoki /12		R	L	Vision
	Pyramid			
	Breast Stroke			
	Isometric Tension			
	Knuckle Grind			
Te Hodoki /15		R	L	Vision
	Opening Lotus			
	Prayer to Heaven			
	Elbow Pressure			
	Takagi Yoshin Omote Gyaku			
	Moving the Bail of Rice			

Aruki waza /6			
Neko Aruki		Kou Aruki	
Shinobi Aruki		Hajai Aruki	
Hirai Aruki		Ushiro Aruki	

Self Defense /57	DESCRIPTION	R	L	VISION
Mei Tsuki 1				
Mei Tsuki 2				
Mei Tsuki 3				
Mei Tsuki 4				
Mei Tsuki 5				
Mei Tsuki 6				
Mei Geri 1				
Mei Geri 2				
Mei Geri 3				
Lapel Grab 1				
Lapel Grab 2				
Lapel Grab 3				
Te Hodoki 1				
Te Hodoki 2				
Te Hodoki 3				
Tai Hodoki 1				
Tai Hodoki 2				
Newaza Bridging				
Newaza Scissor Kick				
Kanji /42				

Nin, Bu, Jin, Po, Do, Jutsu, Ki, Kara, Hou, Shi, Jo, Kan, Sha, Ju, Go, Koshi, Hiji, Hiza, Te, Tai, Ashi
Randori: 60 include weapons
Total Score /213 = %

Notes:

Overall: P / F Signed: _____ Date: _____

Student Test Form

Full Name: _____
Current Rank: 4th kyu
Requested Rank: 3rd kyu
Total Training Hours: _____

Taihenjutsu Ukemi Gata /18		R	L	Vision
Zenpo Ryoho				
Koho				
Sayu yoko zenpo				
Zenpo Kaiten				
Koho Kaiten				
Yoko Kaiten				
Etiquette /2				
	Belt Tying			
	Opening/Closing			
Kamae /12				
Seiza		Ichimonji		
Fudoza		Doko		
Shizen		Hoko		
Hicho		Hira		
Bobi		Ihen		
Jumonji		Kosei		
16 Jewels /16				
Fudo		Boshi		
Koppo		Shuto		
Sanshiten		Shikan		
Shishin		Happa		
Shako		Soki		
Shuki		Sokuyaku		
Sokugyaku		Tai		
Kikaku		Ki		
Sanshin no Kata /15		R	L	Vision
	Chi no kata			
	Sui no kata			
	Ka no kata			
	Fu no kata			
	Ku no kata			
Kihon Happo /21		R	L	Vision
	Omote Gyaku			
	Ura Gyaku			
	Omote no Tsuki			

		Ichimonji Kata			
		Jumonji Kata			
		Hicho Kata			
		Oni Kudaki			
Tai Hodoki	**/12**		R	L	Vision
		Pyramid			
		Breast Stroke			
		Isometric Tension			
		Knuckle Grind			
Te Hodoki	**/15**		R	L	Vision
		Opening Lotus			
		Prayer to Heaven			
		Elbow Pressure			
		Takagi Yoshin Omote Gyaku			
		Moving the Bail of Rice			
Aruki waza	**/6**				
Neko Aruki		Kou Aruki			
Shinobi Aruki		Hajai Aruki			
Hirai Aruki		Ushiro Aruki			
Ne Waza	**/24**		R	L	Vision
		Upa			
		Ebi			
		Ura Ebi			
		Yoko Ebi			
		Kame			
		San Kaku			
		Hasami Geri			
		Hasami Bare			
Self Defense	**/75**	DESCRIPTION	R	L	VISION
Mei Tsuki 1					
Mei Tsuki 2					
Mei Tsuki 3					
Mei Tsuki 4					
Mei Tsuki 5					
Mei Tsuki 6					
Mei Tsuki 7					
Mei Geri 1					
Mei Geri 2					
Mei Geri 3					
Mei Geri 4					
Lapel Grab 1					

Lapel Grab 2			
Lapel Grab 3			
Lapel Grab 4			
Te Hodoki 1			
Te Hodoki 2			
Te Hodoki 3			
Te Hodoki 4			
Tai Hodoki 1			
Tai Hodoki 2			
Tai Hodoki 3			
Newaza Bridging			
Newaza Scissor Kick			
Newaza Pyramid			
Brown Belt Stress Test			
Kanji /56			
Nin, Bu, Jin, Po, Do, Jutsu, Ki, Kara, Hou, Shi, Jo, Kan, Sha, Ju, Go, Koshi, Hiji, Hiza, Te, Tai, Ashi, Rei, Makoto, Jin, Yuki, Gi, Meiyo, Chugi			
Randori: 70 include weapons and multiple opponent			
Total Score /272 = %			

Notes:

Overall: P / F   Signed: _____   Date: _____

Student Test Form

Full Name: _____
Current Rank: 3rd kyu
Requested Rank: 2nd kyu
Total Training Hours: _____

Taihenjutsu Ukemi Gata /18		R	L	Vision
Zenpo Ryoho				
Koho				
Sayu yoko zenpo				
Zenpo Kaiten				
Koho Kaiten				
Yoko Kaiten				
Etiquette /2				
	Belt Tying			
	Opening/Closing			
Kamae /12				
Seiza		Ichimonji		
Fudoza		Doko		
Shizen		Hoko		
Hicho		Hira		
Bobi		Ihen		
Jumonji		Kosei		
16 Jewels /16				
Fudo		Boshi		
Koppo		Shuto		
Sanshiten		Shikan		
Shishin		Happa		
Shako		Soki		
Shuki		Sokuyaku		
Sokugyaku		Tai		
Kikaku		Ki		
Sanshin no Kata /15		R	L	Vision
	Chi no kata			
	Sui no kata			
	Ka no kata			
	Fu no kata			
	Ku no kata			
Kihon Happo /24		R	L	Vision
	Omote Gyaku			
	Ura Gyaku			

	Omote no Tsuki			
	Ichimonji Kata			
	Jumonji Kata			
	Hicho Kata			
	Oni Kudaki			
	Musha Dori			
Tai Hodoki /12		R	L	Vision
	Pyramid			
	Breast Stroke			
	Isometric Tension			
	Knuckle Grind			
Te Hodoki /15		R	L	Vision
	Opening Lotus			
	Prayer to Heaven			
	Elbow Pressure			
	Takagi Yoshin Omote Gyaku			
	Moving the Bail of Rice			
Aruki waza /6				
Neko Aruki	Kou Aruki			
Shinobi Aruki	Hajai Aruki			
Hirai Aruki	Ushiro Aruki			
Ne Waza /24		R	L	Vision
	Upa			
	Ebi			
	Ura Ebi			
	Yoko Ebi			
	Kame			
	San Kaku			
	Hasami Geri			
	Hasami Bare			
Nage Waza /51		R	L	Vision
	Ganseki Nage			
	Ganseki Nage Henka (yoko)			
	Ganseki Goshi			
	Harai Goshi			
	O'Soto Gari			
	O'Soto Nage			
	Tomoe Nage			
	Temakura			
	Sui Ryu			
	Yoko Nagare Henka			

	Yoko Nagare Henka 2			
	Yoko Nagare Henka 3 (ushiro)			
	Kata Garuma			
	Double Leg Shot			
	Double Leg Attempt Sprawl			
	Single Leg Grab Jaw Control			
	O' Gyaku Kata			

Self Defense	/84	DESCRIPTION	R	L	VISION
Mei Tsuki 1					
Mei Tsuki 2					
Mei Tsuki 3					
Mei Tsuki 4					
Mei Tsuki 5					
Mei Tsuki 6					
Mei Tsuki 7					
Mei Tsuki 8					
Mei Geri 1					
Mei Geri 2					
Mei Geri 3					
Mei Geri 4					
Mei Geri 5					
Lapel Grab 1					
Lapel Grab 2					
Lapel Grab 3					
Lapel Grab 4					
Te Hodoki 1					
Te Hodoki 2					
Te Hodoki 3					
Te Hodoki 4					
Tai Hodoki 1					
Tai Hodoki 2					
Tai Hodoki 3					
Newaza Bridging					
Newaza Scissor Kick					
Newaza Pyramid					
Newaza Reverse Shrimp					
Kanji /72					
Nin, Bu, Jin, Po, Do, Jutsu, Ki, Kara, Hou, Shi, Jo, Kan, Sha, Ju, Go, Koshi, Hiji, Hiza, Te, Tai, Ashi, Rei, Makoto, Jin, Yuki, Gi, Meiyo, Chugi, Sabaki, Shirabi, Moguri, Hei, In, Yo, Kyo, Jyaku					
Randori: 80 include weapons and multiple opponent					

Total Score /351 = %

Notes:

Overall: P / F   Signed: _____   Date: _____

Student Test Form

Full Name: _____
Current Rank: 2nd kyu
Requested Rank: 1st kyu
Total Training Hours: _____

Taihenjutsu Ukemi Gata /18		R	L	Vision
Zenpo Ryoho				
Koho				
Sayu yoko zenpo				
Zenpo Kaiten				
Koho Kaiten				
Yoko Kaiten				
Etiquette /2				
	Belt Tying			
	Opening/Closing			
Kamae /12				
Seiza		Ichimonji		
Fudoza		Doko		
Shizen		Hoko		
Hicho		Hira		
Bobi		Ihen		
Jumonji		Kosei		
16 Jewels /16				
Fudo		Boshi		
Koppo		Shuto		
Sanshiten		Shikan		
Shishin		Happa		
Shako		Soki		
Shuki		Sokuyaku		
Sokugyaku		Tai		
Kikaku		Ki		
Sanshin no Kata /15		R	L	Vision
	Chi no kata			
	Sui no kata			
	Ka no kata			
	Fu no kata			
	Ku no kata			
Kihon Happo /24		R	L	Vision
	Omote Gyaku			
	Ura Gyaku			
	Omote no Tsuki			

	Ichimonji Kata			
	Jumonji Kata			
	Hicho Kata			
	Oni Kudaki			
	Musha Dori			
Tai Hodoki /12		R	L	Vision
	Pyramid			
	Breast Stroke			
	Isometric Tension			
	Knuckle Grind			
Te Hodoki /15		R	L	Vision
	Opening Lotus			
	Prayer to Heaven			
	Elbow Pressure			
	Takagi Yoshin Omote Gyaku			
	Moving the Bail of Rice			
Aruki waza /6				
Neko Aruki	Kou Aruki			
Shinobi Aruki	Hajai Aruki			
Hirai Aruki	Ushiro Aruki			
Ne Waza /24		R	L	Vision
	Upa			
	Ebi			
	Ura Ebi			
	Yoko Ebi			
	Kame			
	San Kaku			
	Hasami Geri			
	Hasami Bare			
Nage Waza /51		R	L	Vision
	Ganseki Nage			
	Ganseki Nage Henka (yoko)			
	Ganseki Goshi			
	Harai Goshi			
	O'Soto Gari			
	O'Soto Nage			
	Tomoe Nage			
	Temakura			
	Sui Ryu			
	Yoko Nagare Henka			
	Yoko Nagare Henka 2			

		R	L	Vision
	Yoko Nagare Henka 3 (ushiro)			
	Kata Garuma			
	Double Leg Shot			
	Double Leg Attempt Sprawl			
	Single Leg Grab Jaw Control			
	O' Gyaku Kata			
Buki Waza /157		R	L	Vision
	Shuriken Jutsu Nage 1 /9			
	Shuriken Jutsu Nage 2 /9			
	Shuriken Jutsu Nage 3 /9			
	Shuriken Jutsu Nage 4 /9			
	Kuji Kiri /9			
	Taihen jutsu with sword fwd#1 /2			
	Taihen jutsu with sword fwd#2 /2			
	Taihen jutsu with sword rwd#1 /2			
	Taihen jutsu with sword rwd#2 /2			
	Slap Parry against Skeeti /3			
	Overhead Block agianst Men Kiri /3			
	High Press Block and clear /3			
	hanbo basic pattern /40			
	Hanbo Jutsu Oni Kudaki /3			
	Hanbo Jutsu Tsuki Iri /3			
	Rouko Shoko Bo Uchi Waza Kata /40			
	tanto jutsu 8 count koto ryu kata /3			
	manriki gusari hachi jin no muashi /3			
	manriki gusari ura hachi jin no muashi /3			
Self Defense /93	**DESCRIPTION**	R	L	VISION
Mei Tsuki 1				
Mei Tsuki 2				
Mei Tsuki 3				
Mei Tsuki 4				
Mei Tsuki 5				
Mei Tsuki 6				

Mei Tsuki 7				
Mei Tsuki 8				
Mei Tsuki 9				
Mei Geri 1				
Mei Geri 2				
Mei Geri 3				
Mei Geri 4				
Mei Geri 5				
Lapel Grab 1				
Lapel Grab 2				
Lapel Grab 3				
Lapel Grab 4				
Te Hodoki 1				
Te Hodoki 2				
Te Hodoki 3				
Te Hodoki 4				
Tai Hodoki 1				
Tai Hodoki 2				
Tai Hodoki 3				
Tai Hodoki 4				
Newaza Bridging				
Newaza Scissor Kick				
Newaza Pyramid				
Newaza Reverse Shrimp				
Newaza Scissor Sweep				
Kanji /90				
Nin, Bu, Jin, Po, Do, Jutsu, Ki, Kara, Hou, Shi, Jo, Kan, Sha, Ju, Go, Koshi, Hiji, Hiza, Te, Tai, Ashi, Rei, Makoto, Jin, Yuki, Gi, Meiyo, Chugi, Sabaki, Shirabi, Moguri, Hei, In, Yo, Kyo, Jyaku, Waza, Chi, Sui, Ka, Fu, Ken, Ken, Ai, Hodoki				
Randori: 90 include weapons and multiple opponent				
Total Score /535 = %				

Notes:

Overall: P / F   Signed:_____   Date: _____

Student Test Form

Full Name: _____
Current Rank: 1st kyu
Requested Rank: Shodan
Total Training Hours: _____

Taihenjutsu Ukemi Gata /18		R	L	Vision
Zenpo Ryoho				
Koho				
Sayu yoko zenpo				
Zenpo Kaiten				
Koho Kaiten				
Yoko Kaiten				
Etiquette /2				
	Belt Tying			
	Opening/Closing			
Kamae /12				
Seiza		Ichimonji		
Fudoza		Doko		
Shizen		Hoko		
Hicho		Hira		
Bobi		Ihen		
Jumonji		Kosei		
16 Jewels /16				
Fudo		Boshi		
Koppo		Shuto		
Sanshiten		Shikan		
Shishin		Happa		
Shako		Soki		
Shuki		Sokuyaku		
Sokugyaku		Tai		
Kikaku		Ki		
Sanshin no Kata /15		R	L	Vision
	Chi no kata			
	Sui no kata			
	Ka no kata			
	Fu no kata			
	Ku no kata			
Kihon Happo /24		R	L	Vision
	Omote Gyaku			
	Ura Gyaku			
	Omote no Tsuki			

		Ichimonji Kata			
		Jumonji Kata			
		Hicho Kata			
		Oni Kudaki			
		Musha Dori			
Tai Hodoki	**/12**		R	L	Vision
		Pyramid			
		Breast Stroke			
		Isometric Tension			
		Knuckle Grind			
Te Hodoki	**/15**		R	L	Vision
		Opening Lotus			
		Prayer to Heaven			
		Elbow Pressure			
		Takagi Yoshin Omote Gyaku			
		Moving the Bail of Rice			
Aruki waza	**/6**				
Neko Aruki		Kou Aruki			
Shinobi Aruki		Hajai Aruki			
Hirai Aruki		Ushiro Aruki			
Ne Waza	**/24**		R	L	Vision
		Upa			
		Ebi			
		Ura Ebi			
		Yoko Ebi			
		Kame			
		San Kaku			
		Hasami Geri			
		Hasami Bare			
Nage Waza	**/51**		R	L	Vision
		Ganseki Nage			
		Ganseki Nage Henka (yoko)			
		Ganseki Goshi			
		Harai Goshi			
		O'Soto Gari			
		O'Soto Nage			
		Tomoe Nage			
		Temakura			
		Sui Ryu			
		Yoko Nagare Henka			
		Yoko Nagare Henka 2			

		R	L	Vision
	Yoko Nagare Henka 3 (ushiro)			
	Kata Garuma			
	Double Leg Shot			
	Double Leg Attempt Sprawl			
	Single Leg Grab Jaw Control			
	O' Gyaku Kata			
Buki Waza /157		R	L	Vision
	Shuriken Jutsu Nage 1 /9			
	Shuriken Jutsu Nage 2 /9			
	Shuriken Jutsu Nage 3 /9			
	Shuriken Jutsu Nage 4 /9			
	Kuji Kiri /9			
	Taihen jutsu with sword fwd#1 /2			
	Taihen jutsu with sword fwd#2 /2			
	Taihen jutsu with sword rwd#1 /2			
	Taihen jutsu with sword rwd#2 /2			
	Slap Parry against Skeeti /3			
	Overhead Block agianst Men Kiri /3			
	High Press Block and clear /3			
	hanbo basic pattern /40			
	Hanbo Jutsu Oni Kudaki /3			
	Hanbo Jutsu Tsuki Iri /3			
	Rouko Shoko Bo Uchi Waza Kata /40			
	tanto jutsu 8 count koto ryu kata /3			
	manriki gusari hachi jin no muashi /3			
	manriki gusari ura hachi jin no muashi /3			
Self Defense /105	**DESCRIPTION**	R	L	VISION
Mei Tsuki 1				
Mei Tsuki 2				
Mei Tsuki 3				
Mei Tsuki 4				
Mei Tsuki 5				
Mei Tsuki 6				

Mei Tsuki 7			
Mei Tsuki 8			
Mei Tsuki 9			
Mei Tsuki 10			
Mei Geri 1			
Mei Geri 2			
Mei Geri 3			
Mei Geri 4			
Mei Geri 5			
Mei Geri 6			
Lapel Grab 1			
Lapel Grab 2			
Lapel Grab 3			
Lapel Grab 4			
Lapel Grab 5			
Te Hodoki 1			
Te Hodoki 2			
Te Hodoki 3			
Te Hodoki 4			
Tai Hodoki 1			
Tai Hodoki 2			
Tai Hodoki 3			
Tai Hodoki 4			
Tai Hodoki 5			
Newaza Bridging			
Newaza Scissor Kick			
Newaza Pyramid			
Newaza Reverse Shrimp			
Newaza Scissor Sweep			
Kanji /110			
Nin, Bu, Jin, Po, Do, Jutsu, Ki, Kara, Hou, Shi, Jo, Kan, Sha, Ju, Go, Koshi, Hiji, Hiza, Te, Tai, Ashi, Rei, Makoto, Jin, Yuki, Gi, Meiyo, Chugi, Sabaki, Shirabi, Moguri, Hei, In, Yo, Kyo, Jyaku, Waza, Chi, Sui, Ka, Fu, Ken, Ken, Ai, Hodoki, Ryu, Tora, Nagare, Take, Zen, Shugyo, Sensei, Shidoshi, Shihan, Soke			
Randori: 100 include weapons and multiple opponent			
Total Score /567 = %			

Notes:

Overall: P / F   Signed: _____ Date: _____

Manufactured by Amazon.ca
Acheson, AB